Internet Guide for College-Bound Students

Kenneth E. Hartman

For free updates, visit the College Board Web site at http://www.collegeboard.org

College Entrance Examination Board
New York

Founded in 1900, the College Board is a national, nonprofit membership association of schools, colleges, and other educational organizations working together to help students succeed in the transition from school to college. The Board meets the diverse needs of schools, colleges, educators, students, and parents through the development of standards of excellence; by providing programs and services in guidance, assessment, admission, placement, financial aid, and teaching and learning; and by conducting forums, research, and public policy activities. In all of its work, the Board promotes universal access to high standards of learning, equity of opportunity, and sufficient financial support so that every student has the opportunity to succeed in college and work.

In all of its book publishing activities the College Board endeavors to present the works of authors who are well qualified to write with authority on the subject at hand, and to present accurate and timely information. However, the opinions, interpretations, and conclusions of the authors are their own and do not necessarily represent those of the College Board; nothing contained herein should be assumed to represent an official position of the College Board, or any of its members.

Copies of this book may be ordered from College Board Publications, Box 886, New York, New York 10101-0886. It may also be ordered online at the College Board Online Store, http://www.collegeboard.org. The price is $14.95.

Editorial inquiries concerning this book should be directed to Guidance Publishing, The College Board, 45 Columbus Avenue, New York, New York 10023-6992.

Library of Congress Catalog Number: 96-71036

ISBN: 0-87447-548-1

Printed in the United States of America

9 8 7 6 5 4 3 2 1

Acknowledgments

Many thanks to my colleagues for contributing their thoughts and expertise—including my friend Bill Harris for his unwavering support of this and other initiatives of mine, as well as Martha Gagnon, David Peterson, Conrad Sharrow, Larry Gladieux, Doug Brooke, Iris Gomez, Rich Koch, Maureen Matheson, and David Collins. Thanks, too, to Luke Bonanomi, Nica Ganley, and Mitchell Berger for their input.

Special thanks to Lynell Shore Engelmyer, my contributing "surfer" and eagle-eye proofreader, and to Carolyn Trager, my editor, for assisting and believing in this book.

Dedication

To my wife and best friend, Marti, for doing double duty with the kids while this book was being written, and for her generosity in sharing the family phone line.

Contents

Chapter 1

Setting Out on the Internet

It's happening as you read this page. Colleges and universities across the country—and around the world—are racing to get information about their institutions on the Internet. At the start of 1996, nearly three-quarters of the colleges in the United States, both two-year and four-year, were on the Internet. By 1999, or sooner, all collegiate institutions are expected to be online. Colleges recognize the power and ability of the Internet or "Net" to provide not only vital information and services to enrolled students and faculty, but also to recruit prospective students.

The result of this rapid move into cyberspace is that college-bound students can now tap into vast amounts of insightful information and expertise that were either not available or hard to find in the past. But with nearly 500,000 home pages or locations on the Internet and 300 to 500 new pages created each day—some helpful, some not—the information highway can be difficult to navigate. Only those who know what to look for and where to find it will get the full benefits of this electronic treasure chest. That's why this book was written—to give you direct routes to locations that can help you:

- choose a college
- find out about financial aid and scholarships
- exchange information with other students
- contact college administrators and faculty
- apply to college via the Web
- explore majors and careers

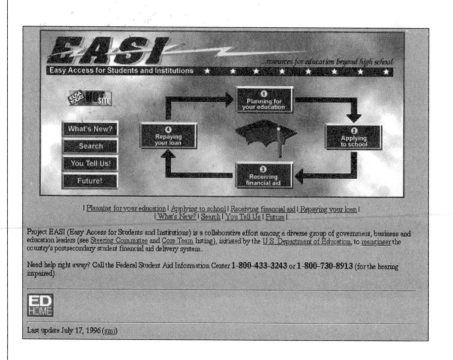

| Planning for your education | Applying to school | Receiving financial aid | Repaying your loan |
| What's New? | Search | You Tell Us | Future |

Project EASI (Easy Access for Students and Institutions) is a collaborative effort among a diverse group of government, business and education leaders (see Steering Committee and Core Team listing), initiated by the U.S. Department of Education, to reengineer the country's postsecondary student financial aid delivery system.

Need help right away? Call the Federal Student Aid Information Center 1-800-433-3243 or 1-800-730-8913 (for the hearing impaired).

Last update July 17, 1996 (gmj)

Six Basic Net Facts

Net Fact # 1   Net Prep Pays

Lewis Carroll, author of *Alice in Wonderland*, recognized the importance of a plan. It was Carroll who said, through the character Alice, "Cheshire Cat, would you tell me, please, which way I ought to go from here?"

"That depends a good deal on where you want to get to," said the cat.

"Oh, I do not much care where," said Alice.

"Then it does not matter which way you go," said the cat.

Unlike Alice, you and most other college-bound students do care "where you want to get to." You want to avoid getting lost and frustrated on the Internet and want to be sure you end up in the right place each time you get on the Net to explore colleges, financial aid, or career possibilities. The best way to do that is to set out with a clear Net Plan. That's what this book is all about. Using it as a guide, you'll find out where to locate vital information and, just as important, you'll learn what questions to ask yourself and others.

One of the key tools for making a sound Net Plan is Dr. H's World Wide Web Worksheet, a handy guide to navigating any college's Web site. It can save you a lot of time and

4 money—not only on the cost of online charges but also on the price you'll eventually pay for any college. (See Chapter 3 for details.)

Net Fact # 2   The Greater the Persistence, the Greater the Rewards

To get to the sweetest part of a peach, you first have to peel away the skin and tart outer layer of the fruit. Searching the Internet is a little like that. You often have to peel away several layers of Web pages to get to a location that satisfies your college-information appetite. This book is designed to give you shortcuts to your destination, but until the Internet is better organized, you'll have to be persistent in devising and pursuing search strategies.

Net Fact # 3   Not All College Net Sites Are Created Equal

Some colleges—big and small, public and private—have given a lot of forethought and spent a great deal of money to develop Web sites that are innovative, lively, and fact filled. The best Web sites are loaded and updated regularly with valuable information and resources, just waiting for you to tap into once you know where to look. Other colleges have done the job too quickly in an effort to get something, anything, online and it takes a little more ingenuity to make good use of their sites. In either case, this book can help you develop the skills and insights needed to get the most out of any college Web site.

Net Fact # 4   The College Home Page Is Only a Starting Point

The key to any successful online search is to go beyond the obvious or "official" information about a college and financial aid. Often the most useful information is found in the "unofficial" online areas of a Web site. There are tips throughout this book to help you to find and analyze both official and unofficial information.

Net Fact # 5   All Information Has Some Value

A comprehensive Net search will lead you to a wealth of information, both factual and subjective. It's up to you to weigh the value of what you learn. Do you decide, for example, not to apply to a college that interests you because 10 or 12 enrolled students replied negatively to an e-mail questionnaire you sent them? Do you move a college that was low on your list up toward the top because the student newspaper is livelier and more appealing than any others you have seen?

Chapter 7 gives you tips on how to analyze the information you're collecting to put the facts, along with your subjective impressions, into perspective.

Net Fact # 6   ## You're Breaking New Ground on the Internet

By exploring the ideas, methods, and approaches outlined in this book, you will become a true Internet pioneer. You'll get information more quickly and go beyond a college's admission and financial aid office for answers to your questions. You'll be able to communicate directly by e-mail with faculty, enrolled students, alumni, or the campus security officer. You're on the cutting edge, so don't be surprised when other people ask, "Where in the world did you find that information?"

The Internet lets you do your college research a lot more quickly than you could only a few years ago and gives you the chance to gather a much wider range of information. Used wisely, with a good basic plan plus a sense of adventure, it can be an invaluable guide to making sound college choices and finding funds to pay for your education. Read on to find out how you can make the most of this new electronic resource.

http://www.utexas.edu/world/lecture/

World Lecture Hall

The World Lecture Hall (WLH) contains links to pages created by faculty worldwide who are using the Web to deliver class materials. For example, you will find course syllabi, assignments, lecture notes, exams, class calendars, multimedia textbooks, etc.

Here's a form to add your materials. For additions to the WLH, see What's New (25 June 96).

Basic Facts About the Internet

Timeline

1950s **The Beginning**

The Internet was developed in the late 1950s by the U.S. Pentagon. It began as a small network of computers that, in the event of a nuclear attack, could maintain a communications link between important military locations. At that point there were fewer than a thousand users.

1960s and 1970s **Growing Up and Going to College**

Less than a decade after the Internet was created, several

major research universities took the Pentagon's network and improved its performance, to make it quicker and easier to share research results and other scholarly information. Because few people had personal computers, which were still pretty slow and complicated to use, the Internet remained a tool for specialists —fewer than 5,000 of them at the end of the 1970s.

1980s — Becoming the Information Superhighway

By the early 1980s, the National Science Foundation recognized the scientific potential of this network and spent several billion dollars to enhance and expand it. Since then, tens of thousands of organizations throughout the world have joined the Internet, each branching off to provide millions of individuals, like you, with access to the "Information Superhighway." The Internet, like a major highway with thousands of on- and off-ramps to different cities and towns, lets you travel to different sites around the world, each offering a unique assortment of resources and information. The Internet highway works because every computer in the world uses the same standard language, called Internet Protocol, or IP, to communicate.

1990s — Creating a Language of Its Own

Early users of the Internet shared e-mail and data using software such as FTP (File Transfer Protocol), Telnet (which enables a single computer to tap into a remote computer network), and Gopher (a text-based program that locates and retrieves information on the Net). If the Internet had remained this text-only system, you wouldn't be reading this book today.

Adding Multimedia

The big change came in the early 1990s with the development of the World Wide Web, which uses a programming language called HTML (hypertext markup language) to access files, referred to as pages. HTML eliminated the need to understand complicated software or to be a computer scientist to use the Internet. Now, just about anyone can easily navigate the Internet and create a Web page for others to read and respond to.

Getting Connected— the Internet Equation

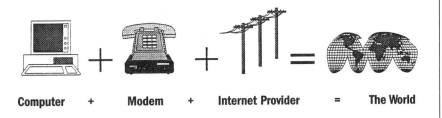

| Computer | + | Modem | + | Internet Provider | = | The World |

Most computers sold today come equipped with the basic hardware and software you need to connect to the Internet. The following are suggested hardware requirements:

Hardware	Minimum	Better	Ideal
PC/CPU	386	486	Pentium
Mac/CPU	68030	68040	Power Mac
RAM	4Mb	8Mb	16Mb-plus
Hard drive	350Mb	1 Gig	1.6 Gig-plus
CD-ROM	2X-speed	4X-speed	6X-speed
Modem	14,400 bps	28,800 bps	ISDN

To take full advantage of the Internet—and the World Wide Web—your computer should also be equipped with:

- High-resolution color monitor
- Sound card for playing sound and videos—but don't be daunted if you don't have this component because you'll still have access to lots of information.

Speed Counts

The key piece of hardware is a modem, short for modulator/demodulator, which links your computer with the Internet via your phone line. If your computer doesn't come equipped with a modem, you'll need to buy one that is compatible with your system.

When choosing and using a modem, the bottom line is speed. The faster the modem, the less time you'll have to

spend on the Net locating and retrieving information. And
the less time you spend online, the less money you're going
to have to pay the company that provides you with access to
the Internet.

While you can access the Web with a 2,400 baud modem,
the suggested minimum modem speed is 14.4 bps. 28.8 bps is
even better, so start with that if possible.

Ways of Connecting

Option #1 **Online Service Company**

The simplest and currently the most popular connection
between a home computer and the Net is through one of the
major online service companies.

Online services	Benefits	Drawbacks
America Online	Easy to use; free trial	Monthly fee for limit-
Prodigy	period; full access to	ed number of hours
CompuServe	Internet; wide range	of use; hourly charge
Microsoft Network	of information and	beyond minimum
Genie	services; nationwide	
	local access (normally	
	toll free); ability to	
	create personal home	
	pages	

12

Each of these companies gives you a free trial period, usually 10 hours of online time, to use its services—anything from games, movie reviews, and news of the day to online help with homework, as well as entry to the Internet—before signing up. Location is no barrier. If you decide to take your laptop computer with you on vacation, you just have to check the online company's directory to find out the local/toll-free access phone number to dial into the company's computer or "server."

The online service companies all have similar pricing plans, as you can see in the Service Providers Chart on page 20. You may want to check out several before deciding which one, if any, you want to subscribe to. Keep in mind, too, that those hourly charges can add up to a hefty bill if you're searching the Internet without a clear idea of how to find what you're looking for or if you're using a slow modem.

Option #2   Internet Service Provider

An alternative that you might want to consider is a national or local Internet service provider (ISP).

While ISPs generally don't provide the icons, graphics, and organized subject areas that you'll get with an online company, they do offer full Internet access. Many of them have a flat monthly charge for unlimited connection time, which may be an economical option if you plan to spend a lot of time on the Net. The Service Providers Chart includes some typical fees.

The Consumer's Checklist on page 21 gives you basic guidelines to follow when selecting an ISP. Most important, you want to be certain that the ISP you choose can guarantee you fast service when you want it—anytime, day or night.

National ISPs	Benefits	Drawbacks
Netcom	Flat rate offered by	Limited online
AlterNet	some; nationwide	services
AT&T	access; 24-hour tech-	
MCI	nical support	
Sprint		
Local ISPs		
See yellow pages, ads	Rate may be lower	Limited technical
in local newspapers,	than national	service; access phone
or go to	company	number may be only
http://www.thelist.com		for local calls

Option #3 **Dedicated Connection**

The third alternative, a dedicated connection, offers high speed at a high price, and is more commonly used by businesses and institutions than by individuals. It provides a direct route to the Internet via a specially installed T-1 or T-3 telephone line, which can transmit information at a rate 50 times faster than a 28.8 bps modem.

Some local telephone and television cable companies are

beginning to offer their commercial and residential customers a type of dedicated connection called an ISDN, but the monthly charge and start-up costs are still too high for most individual users.

Dedicated connection	Benefits	Drawbacks
Integrated Service Digital Network (ISDN)	50 times faster than 28.8 bps; doesn't tie up telephone; unlimited access to the Net	Expensive to set up; special equipment needed; costs $40 to $150 per month
T-1 or T-3	Fastest way to travel on the Net; unlimited access to the Net	Costs $1,000 to $2,000 per month

Start-up fees for a T-1 or T-3 line, plus very high monthly charges, make that option too expensive for personal use at this point. If a computer in your school or library is connected to the Net via a T-1 or T-3 line and you have access to it, make use of it because this is the fastest way to find what you're looking for.

Alumni/Admitted Student Connections

Another Internet-access possibility is your parents' alma mater. Some colleges offer low-cost or free Net connection to alumni. Like commercial service providers, they provide

the necessary software and a local access phone number that
lets you dial in to their computer, which connects you to the
Internet. There are also colleges—Michigan State University,
for example—that offer free Net access, including a personal
e-mail address, to high school students who have been
admitted to the college.

Internet Tools to Be Aware of

Gopher

Gopher (named after the mascot at the University of
Minnesota, where the system was developed in the 1980s) is
one of the tools you can use to find and retrieve Internet
text documents. You simply type in the name of the subject
(for example, Abraham Lincoln) and the Gopher will do a
global search for any document online that makes reference
to your subject.

Few people still rely on Gopher as a tool for getting
around the Internet (college faculty and academic
researchers are the exception). Instead, many Internet users
are turning to the browser found on the World Wide Web
to retrieve information. But it's a good idea to be familiar
with as many search tools as possible to widen your access
to information.

Telnet

Like Gopher, Telnet was used more widely in the past than it is now to access information from remote locations, for example, the computerized archives at the Library of Congress in Washington, D.C. But with the growth of the World Wide Web, Net users have less need for this tool.

FTP (File Transfer Protocol)

FTP is a Net tool that enables you to transfer or "download" files, including video and audio files, from a Web site to your computer.

Communicating with Other People

A good way to find out about a college or career is to talk to the people who know it best:

- students who are currently enrolled
- alumni
- faculty who develop the courses you're interested in
- administrators who make admission decisions
- working professionals in fields that interest you

What better way to find out about financial aid than by talking with experts in the field? The Internet lets you carry on a conversation with one person or hundreds of people at one time. Here are some of the ways to do that.

E-Mail

E-mail is a tool for sending messages from one user to another via an electronic network. Anyone who has a Net address (assigned and managed by your Internet provider) can be contacted with a question or a request for information. In Chapter 3 you'll find out not only how to find and use a VIP's e-mail address, but what to ask the person you're contacting.

Newsgroups (Sometimes Called Usenet or Discussion Groups)

Newsgroups are electronic message boards where you can post inquiries, comments, and/or suggestions on a topic of common interest. There are thousands of newsgroups on the Net. Each newsgroup has a name ("college admission," for example) and usually has a number of specialized categories within it, such as "private colleges in New York State." You can read recent messages posted to the newsgroup or browse through messages on the topic from weeks or months earlier. Chapter 5 includes tips on how to make good use of newsgroups to gather firsthand information on colleges and financial aid.

Mailing Lists (Sometimes Called Listservs and Discussion Lists)

A mailing list is a one-to-many form of e-mail communication about a specific subject area. It works something like a magazine or newspaper subscription. The difference is that a mailing list subscription is free and the "news" and "articles" are by the people who receive and respond to the e-mail messages. Once you subscribe, you will receive all messages sent to that particular mailing list, which gives you a chance to discuss issues in the field, ask for advice from other sub-scribers, get information, and even coordinate action. Mailing lists usually have a national or international member-ship, giving you the chance to draw on the collective know-ledge and experience of thousands of people. See Chapter 5 for information on how to find and subscribe to the mailing list(s) that can help you.

Chat Areas (Technically Called Internet Relay Chat or IRC)

A chat area, or room, is the Internet's version of the confer-ence phone call. Basically, it's a meeting place on the Net where people can have an electronic conversation in "real time" about choosing a major, saving for college, or any other topic of mutual interest. Everyone at that location at that time can participate by keying and sending a message. For more details about how this Net tool can help you get important information and helpful advice instantaneously from a wide network of people, see Chapter 5.

The Web, as it's called, is the newest, fastest growing, and most popular spot on the Internet because it is the only Net site that offers information in multimedia: text, graphics, video pictures, and sound. The Web organizes and links information on the Internet so that all you have to do is click on a word or phrase (called hypertext) and you're instantly at the site that has information on that subject.

Not surprisingly, you'll find the Web to be your best source of information on colleges, financial aid, and careers. In Chapter 3, you'll learn what the basic components of a home page are and how to use a specially designed Web worksheet to find and analyze the wealth of information waiting for you on the Web.

Service Providers Chart

Commercial Online Service Providers

Service	Fee/Additional hourly charge	Phone number
America Online	$9.95 monthly for 5 hours plus $2.95 for each additional hour; or $20 monthly for 20 hours plus $2.95 for each additional hour	800-827-6364
CompuServe	$9.95 monthly for 5 hours plus $2.95 for each additional hour; or $24.95 monthly for 20 hours plus $1.95 for each additional hour	800-848-8199
Microsoft Network	$4.95 monthly for 3 hours plus $2.95 for each additional hour; or $19.95 monthly for 30 hours plus $2.95 for each additional hour	800-386-5550
Prodigy	$9.95 monthly for 5 hours plus $2.95 for each additional hour; or $29.95 monthly for 30 hours plus $2.95 for each additional hour	800-776-3449

National Internet Service Providers (SLIP/PPP)

GNN	$14.95 monthly for 20 hours plus $1.95 for each additional hour	800-819-6112
Netcom	$25 for initial setup plus $19.95 monthly for first 40 hours of primetime use plus $2 for each additional hour of primetime use	800-353-6600
Pipeline USA	$19.95 monthly for unlimited use	800-453-7473

Rates are current as of July 1996.

Consumer's Checklist

Does the ISP provide:

- ☐ 24-hour/7-day phone service for technical help?
- ☐ Multiple access points or "POPs"? Local POPs? National POPs? Toll-free?
- ☐ 28.8 bps and higher connection? How many local access numbers at 28.8 bps and higher?
- ☐ Personal home pages? Number and size permitted?
- ☐ Price? Hourly or flat fee? Charge per e-mail?
- ☐ Software included? FTP? Gopher? Newsgroups? WWW browser?
- ☐ Mechanism included for parental control of access to the Internet?

Name of ISP	Features	Cost

Chapter 3

World Wide Web —One-Stop Shopping for College Information

Imagine buying a $100,000 automobile based on listening to the car dealer's comments about it, reading the manufacturer's brochure, talking with a few people who know something about the car but never owned that model, and taking one quick test-drive around a track designed by the dealer. The car, by the way, comes with no warranty or guarantee of satisfaction.

That may sound far-fetched, but it's not too different from the way many college-bound students and their parents decide to spend $100,000 or more for a college education. In many cases, the decision to go to a particular college is based on the "reputation" of the institution, the advice of a college counselor and/or friend of the family, a viewbook and video from the college, a brief tour of the campus, and an even briefer interview with an admission officer.

Relying on meager information and acting on impulse may account for the fact that nearly one-third of all undergraduate students decide, after a year or two, that they've made a poor choice and transfer to another college. An even larger percentage drop out and never complete their college education. But you can easily avoid being part of those statistics. Here's how.

Using the Internet to Find the College That's Right for You

The Internet is a vast storehouse of information, advice, and opinions about colleges. It's there for you to explore as fully and as often as you want—a resource that makes the job of choosing the right college much easier. This book is your guide to:

- where to look
- what to look for
- what questions to ask

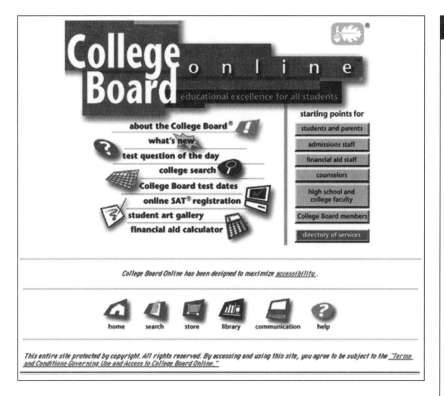

A Quick Look at How Other Students Are Using the Internet

Looking for the Best in Biology

Mary, a high school junior, wants to major in biology in college. After discussing her options with her school counselor, she decides to use the Internet to learn more about five colleges at the top of her list. Her first stop is the home page of a major state university, which leads her to the biology department's Web site.

Getting Firsthand Answers

She zeroes in on the e-mail addresses for biology faculty and student members of the Biology Club, then does a random e-mail survey of matriculated biology students to get their responses to her five basic questions.

1. How accessible are your instructors?
2. What percentage of your classes are taught by graduate students?
3. What opportunities for research are available to undergraduates?
4. Would you recommend the department to a prospective student?
5. What is/was the average enrollment of your freshman-year biology classes?

Checking Out the Faculty

Mary also does a quick evaluation of the biology department teaching staff by scanning the following information about each:

- stated research interests
- degrees and other professional accomplishments
- recent publications

She does a little further research by reading a few articles listed that sound particularly interesting. Since they're linked by hypertext, she just clicks on a title to bring it up online rather than going to the library. Mary does the same Internet investigation of four other colleges that she thinks might be good choices for her. These first steps give her useful benchmarks for comparing the merits of the five colleges she's considering, but she'll use the Net again to have e-mail "conversations" with some of the instructors and get inside information about campus social life, what the dorms are like, whether men's and women's athletic facilities are comparable, and other aspects of college life that make the difference between enjoying or just enduring your college years.

Making the Right Decision About Transfer

Daniel, an African American student currently enrolled at a community college, wants to transfer to a university after he completes his freshman year. To get a sense of the racial climate at a particular college that he's considering, he uses the Internet to:

- read back issues of the student newspaper, sorting for articles/opinions on "race relations on campus"
- send a brief questionnaire to a number of matriculated African American students, using e-mail addresses found on the college's African American Student Union Web page
- survey recent African American alumni via e-mail (addresses found on the college's African American Alumni Association Web page) about their experiences on that campus
- do an online scan of the "hate crime" statistics compiled by his State Department of Education

The information he gathers will help him decide whether to explore other universities before applying for transfer.

Eyeing the Ivy League

Catherine, a high school sophomore, has her sights set on a specific Ivy League college because of the reputation of its teaching staff. The viewbook lists many Nobel Prize winners among the faculty, but she does a quick online search of the college's Web site and finds out that:

- none of the "star" scholars are scheduled to teach any undergraduate courses in the coming year
- nearly half of the instructors slated to teach freshman-level courses are either adjunct professors, graduate students, or listed as "TBA" (to be announced)

To gather more in-depth information, Catherine uses the Net to:

- send e-mail to the instructors of five freshman-level courses, requesting a syllabus and required reading list from each
- read the course and instructor evaluations that are posted on the personal home page of a graduating senior at that institution

Casting a Wide Net

Marti is a high school junior who wants to find out as much

as she can about many colleges before narrowing her search. Since her school encourages students to use its Internet Web site, she decides to set up a BBS (Bulletin Board Service), which puts her in touch with students anywhere in the world who are interested in sharing facts, advice, and opinions about colleges they're planning to attend or in which they are already enrolled. Since students can post messages anonymously, some include a lot of details about their financial circumstances, academic strengths and weaknesses, experiences with campus administrators, etc., which gives Marti a broader perspective than she could get from viewbooks or college directories. Here's a partial list of the kind of information she is collecting about a wide range of colleges:

- amount and type of financial aid packages offered
- average SAT, ACT, and GRE scores of admitted students
- job and graduate school prospects
- life in the residence halls
- pros and cons of meal plans
- campus security—or lack of

In the coming year, Marti plans to work with her school to add a real-time chat room to the school's Web site and create a listserv for all graduating high school seniors in her state. The chat room will let Marti and other participating students have electronic conversations and exhange ideas as immediately as if they were on the telephone. The listserv enables any one of them to send an e-mail message or a comment about a college to hundreds, possibly thousands, of students who are signed on to the list with an e-mail address.

Official vs. Unofficial Information

The brief "case studies" you've just read give you an idea of how to locate and use both "official" and "unofficial" information on the Net to help you make decisions about college. Just to clarify the difference between the two types:

Official

Information provided by the college, typically by the admission office, that is intended to present the institution in as favorable a way as possible. Viewbooks, online or in print form, are an example.

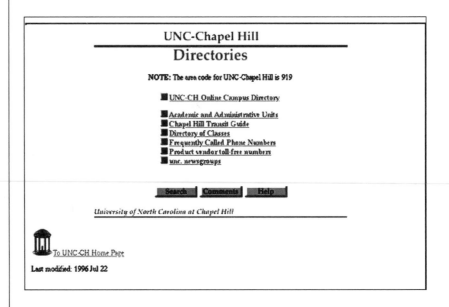

Facts and opinions that come from sources other than a college's administrative staff—for example, student newspapers, student and faculty home pages.

Now let's look at how various Net tools can help you search for the right college.

Web Browser

As you know by now, there's a wealth of information and other resources on the Web. The key that unlocks those treasures is your Web browser—the software provided by your ISP for navigating on the Net. Learning how to use it effectively is a skill you'll want to develop as quickly as you can.

A number of different browsers are available, some better than others, but they all share certain features. The goal is to find and use a browser that offers the widest choice of Net tools, including e-mail, Telnet, or Gopher capability.

Chances are you'll be using one of the following browsers:

- Webcrawler™ (America Online®)
- Explorer™ (Microsoft Network®)
- Spry Mosaic™ (CompuServe®)
- Netscape™ Navigator or Navigator Gold

The last browser on the list is the most widely used at this

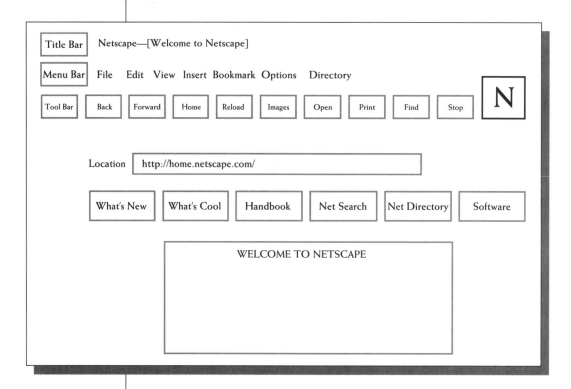

| Title Bar | Netscape—[Welcome to Netscape] |

| Menu Bar | File   Edit   View   Insert   Bookmark   Options   Directory |

| Tool Bar | Back | Forward | Home | Reload | Images | Open | Print | Find | Stop | N

Location   http://home.netscape.com/

| What's New | What's Cool | Handbook | Net Search | Net Directory | Software |

WELCOME TO NETSCAPE

time. The majority of commercial and college Web sites are built to Netscape standards, which means that if you're using a browser other than Netscape, you might not have full access to the site. Here's what Netscape 2.0 looks like and an explanation of a few of its features, each of which is found on other browsers but by other names:

Title, Menu, and Tool Bars

The example above shows the standard Netscape features. The title bar identifies the browser name. The menu and tool bars identify functions and options to help you navigate the Web. If your browser doesn't have e-mail capability, you're going to use the cut and paste option a lot when sending e-mail to VIPs.

Location

This is where you'll type in the address (technically called the Uniform Resource Locator or URL) for the Web site you want to visit. Every site on the Internet has a URL. The URL has three main sections, as shown by the following example:

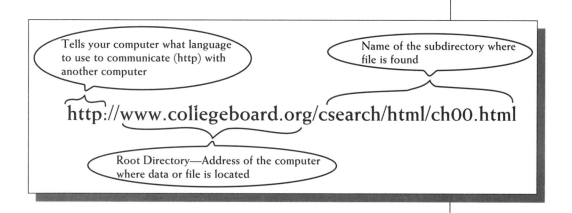

URL is a uniform way of identifying an Internet location in a format that all Web browsers can interpret. For example, no matter what browser you're using, the URL http://www.collegeboard.org takes you to the College Board Web page. The letters "http" (hypertext transport protocol), followed by a colon and two back slashes, indicate a WWW address. If there is additional information in the URL following a back slash at the end of the address, there is a specific subdirectory page at that site. For example, /csearch/html/ch00.html gets you to a location at the College Board's Web site, where you can conduct a college search.

Oops, Where Did It Go?

All the URLs (Web addresses) in the book were checked and double-checked before the book was printed. But URLs are always changing—especially subdirectories.

If your computer can't locate an Internet URL, try:

- checking the URL address to be sure you entered it exactly. Any error or omission in the URL will result in a "Not Found" message
- deleting all subdirectories, entering only the root URL address (home page) and then surfing the site until you locate the file you want. For example:

http://www.collegeboard.org/

Bookmarks

This is one of the most valuable features of any browser. The Bookmark (called "Favorite Place" by AOL, "Hot-List" by others) enables you to save any Web page/URL address you visited for quick reference and return. You'll probably accumulate as many as 100 bookmarks by the end of your college Net search.

Forward

This tool lets you move easily between Web pages.

Go

The browser keeps a history list of places visited during an online session, and you can jump directly to one of those sites.Insert the Web address and the browser will do the rest.

What's New

The sponsor of the browser scans the Net regularly and posts brief descriptions and URL addresses of new Web sites. It's a nice feature for recreational use of the Net but rarely has anything to do with college admission and financial aid.

What's Cool

Similar to "What's New."

Net Search

Browsers contain search engines that enable you to find Web resources by entering key words and phrases. For example, when you type in "financial aid," a brief description of dozens of Web sites pertaining to financial aid (along with their URLs) will appear on your screen.

Where to Find Good Tips on Net Tools— Online and Offline

- *Internet World* (March, 1996, Volume 7, Number 3) published a great evaluation of the major ISPs and their Web browsers.
  http://www.iworld.com
- *Technology & Learning Magazine* (October, 1995, Volume 16, Number 2) is a good source for information on Web browsers and surfing the Web.
- *Multimedia World Magazine* (April, 1996, Volume 3, Number 5) published a good review and ranking of the major Net browsers. Search online (http://www.mmworld.com) for the article entitled "Browser Battle."

Home Pages—Opening the Doors to Information

The home page of a Web site gives you a quick overview of what information and resources are available at that site. The four examples below are typical of what you'll see as you begin your search for official and unofficial information on a specific college.

Once on the Net, the quickest way to find a college's home page is to use your browser to locate one of the following Web sites:

- **Argyle and Navigator Communications**
  http://www.nav.com/OWR/oneworld.html
  Search and link to colleges in over 40 countries
  around the world.
- **Christina DeMello Search**
  http://www.mit.edu:8001/people/cdemello/univ.html
  One of the first and oldest college home page search
  sites. Has won numerous awards in the past two years.
  Over 3,000 colleges in the data base.
- **Colleges and Universities Search**
  http://www.universities.com/
  Nothing fancy as of yet here. Simple home page
  search with over 3,000 colleges in their data base.
- **Global Computing, Inc.**
  http://www.globalcomputing.com/universy.html
  Direct links to the home pages of over 700 American
  universities.
- **University Pages**
  http://isl-garnet.uah.edu/Universities_g/
  Simple search, by state, sponsored by the University
  of Alabama at Huntsville.
- **Yahoo Search** (my personal favorite)
  http://www.yahoo.com/Regional/Countries
  /United_States/Education/Colleges_and_Universities/
  One of the most popular and easy ways to find and
  link to a particular college, along with dozens of
  indices, including the college's e-mail, departments,
  and student clubs.

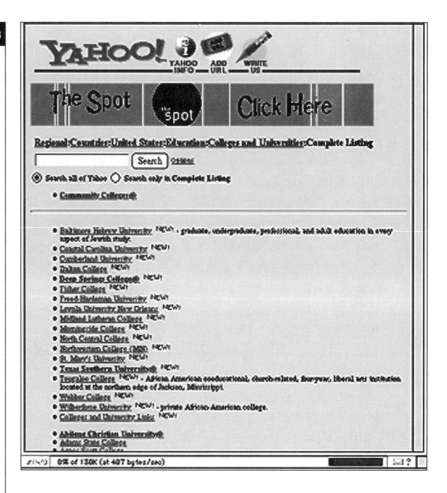

Here are a few sites where you can search for the home page of a community or other two-year college in the United States:

http://www.careermart.com/MMM
    /communitycolleges.html
http://www.mcli.dist.maricopa.edu/cc/
http://www.utexas.edu/world/comcol.html
http://www.sp.utoledo.edu/twoyrcol.html

Geneseo First Look

Academics

Administration

Admissions

Student Life

Libraries

Information Technology

Alumni

What's New

Search Phonebook Links Feedback Index 125th

Questions or comments? Contact our webmaster | text version | Server Statistics

University of Pennsylvania

Historic Preservation

Explore a view:

Faculty & Colleagues Worldwide
Students · Prospective Students
Alumni, Neighbors, Visitors
University Staff

About Penn · Penn Index · Calendar · Search · Help

Contact: webmaster@www.upenn.edu
Certifying Authority: WWW Steering Committee
Last modified: 23 April 1996
URL: http://www.upenn.edu/

Or you can search the Net using the full name of the college or university. Once you've located the college, click on the hypertext name of the institution (typically in blue type) and you're there. Some search sites, like Yahoo, will locate and connect you to different departments, clubs, or sports teams at the college.

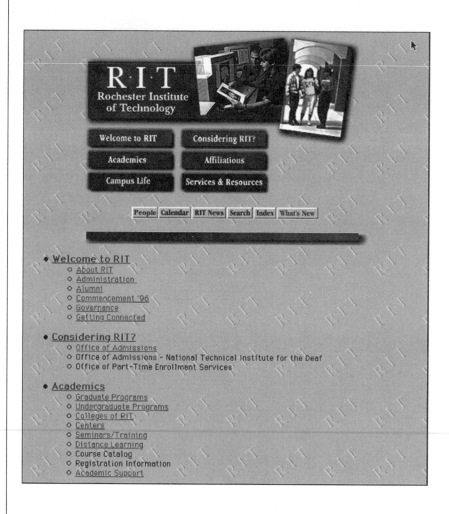

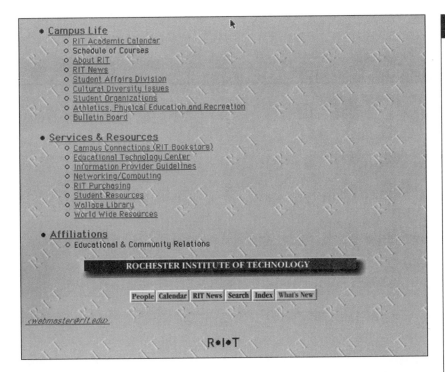

41

Not Sure Which Colleges to Explore?

With more than 3,500 colleges to choose from in the United States and many more around the world, you'll want to narrow the list before gathering in-depth information about specific colleges.

You'll find several sites on the Web (see Top College Searches on the Web, Appendix A) that are good starting points for your initial college search. For free or at little cost, these sites will give you a set of college features from which to choose, among them:

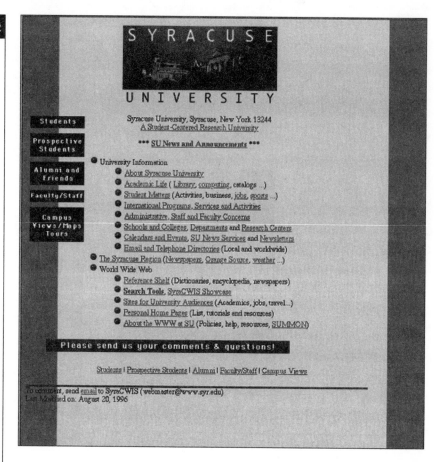

- type of college (two-year, four-year)
- size and setting of college
- geographic location
- housing preference, etc.

When you've entered your preferences, the search program will give you a list of the colleges that most closely match the features you want. Each search site lets you hyperlink directly to the home page of each college on your search list.

Top College Searches on the Web

- **College Board Online**
  http://www.collegeboard.org/csearch/html/ch00.html
  Use the award-winning college search software
  ExPAN online for free to find colleges that match
  your goals and interests. Includes in-depth informa-
  tion about all two-year and four-year colleges in the
  United States, plus the complete text of *The College
  Handbook.*

- **CollegeEdge**
  http://www.collegeedge.com
  Find useful advice and information on researching,
  applying, and going to college. Search alphabetically
  for any college on the WWW. Get your college application essay reviewed by a former Harvard professor.

- **The College Guide**
  http://www.jayi.com/jayi/ACG/CGTOC.html
  This student-oriented site offers electronic links to
  colleges, admission advice, a searchable data base, and
  general information about college life.

- **CollegeNET**
  http://www.collegenet.com
  This is a searchable data base of colleges, scholarship
  opportunities, and academic resources. Offers a comprehensive college/university index with good graphics. Recently has begun offering online application
  processing for "featured schools" only.

- **CollegeTown**
  http://www.ctown.com/

Uses a "campus quad" metaphor to provide space for an admission office, financial aid office, etc. This site provides links to many colleges and offers multimedia "portfolios" for "member" institutions. Many of the services promised are still "under development."

- **CollegeView**
  http://www.collegeview.com
  By combining a data base of 3,300 two- and four-year colleges with multimedia "tours," CollegeView gives students and parents a general overview of a college, plus a direct e-mail option for requesting additional information.

- **CollegeXpress**
  http://www.collegexpress.com
  Search colleges by state, major, and other factors. Take a virtual tour of some colleges and ask their "experts" questions about the college admission process.

- **FishNet**
  http://www.jayi.com/jayi
  Get information on colleges via their college search page; create a profile of yourself to send to colleges; ask questions of their admission expert; get information about paying for college; read a collection of articles about college and the admission process.

- **Internet College Exchange**
  http://www.usmall.com/college/index.html
  With a searchable home page and forums/discussion groups regarding college life, this site mirrors others on this list. In the future, mailing list enrollment and expanded college information will be available. Has received considerable "hot site" recognition from various Web rating organizations.

- **Peterson's Education Center**
  http://www.petersons.com
  Peterson's college data base is available on this home
  page, as is other educational and career information.
- **The Princeton Review**
  http://www.review.com/undergr/best_schools_form.html
  You may search the *Princeton Review's* site by the
  school's name, region, state, size, and cost. The
  Princeton Review also provides you with its rating of
  hundreds of colleges.
- **Resource Pathways College Information Community**
  http://www.sourcepath.com/
  This site offers ranking and "star" evaluations of college admission and financial aid resources, both paper
  based and Internet U.S. News ranking of college
  admission resources.

Special Group Searches

- **Historically Black Colleges and Universities and
  Hispanic Serving Institutions**
  http://www.web.fie.com/web/mol/schlmap.html
  http://www.smart.net/~pope/hbcu/hbculist.html
- **Ivy League Universities**
  http://www.artsci.wustl.edu/~jrdorkin/ivy.html
  Not much here yet, but it's a shortcut for those interested in the most selective colleges in the country.
- **Jesuit Colleges and Universities**
  http://www.ajcunet.edu
  This service will assist you in searching, linking to,
  and requesting an application from Jesuit colleges and
  universities in the United States.

- **National Liberal Arts Colleges**
  http://www.aavc.vassar.edu/libarts.colleges.html
  A list of academic institutions classified by the
  Carnegie Foundation for the Advancement of
  Teaching at national liberal arts colleges.

 guidance and application network
College Information

Use the ExPAN College Information Search to find the right
college for you. By entering specific criteria (geographic location,
enrollment size, majors offered, etc.) you can search a
comprehensive data base of associate and bachelor's degree
granting institutions for the college that best meets your needs.
After searching, you can view a variety of facts and statistics
intended to assist you in your college selection process.

For detailed instructions on how to use the ExPAN College
Information Search, click on the "Help" button at the bottom of
the NEXT screen.

NOTE: A browser that supports tables, such as the Netscape
Navigator, is required to search on and view college
information. You can download the Netscape Navigator directly
from College Board Online, if you wish.

Questions? Problems? Comments? Tell us what you think about
ExPAN College Search.

Coming Soon: Associate and bachelor's level electronic college
APPLICATION

Please select the desired degree level to search on.

1. ○ Associate
2. ◉ Bachelor's
3. ○ Master's
4. ○ Doctoral
5. ○ Professional

Continue

 home   search   store   library   communication   help

How to Get What You Want from Any College Home Page

While college home pages and Web sites in general have some common features, they aren't identical. Some are clear and easy to navigate, hyperlinking you to good information (mostly official), while others are confusing and make you search through screen after screen to find the information and resources you want. For fun, check out MIT's Christina DeMello survey of the best college home pages at:

http://www.mit.edu:8001/people/cdemello/results.html

Don't be daunted, though, because Dr. H's World Wide Web Worksheet gives you a quick, easy system for finding, recording, and assessing the important information and resources—official and unofficial—of any college on the Web. For best results, you'll want to use a separate worksheet for every college you visit on the Web.

How to Use Dr. H's World Wide Web Worksheet

This handy worksheet consists of three sections:

I. General Information
- College Web Site Checklist

II. Specific Information
- About the College
- About Admission

- About Academics
- About Student Life & Services

III. Comments, Special Features, Off-Site Resources

Here's how to use each section:

Start with the College Web Site Checklist to get a quick overview of the basic information each Web site has to offer. Check off the features that interest you, but don't take the time to read through them on your initial overview. You may want to do this for several colleges before delving into specific information and completing a detailed World Wide Web worksheet for a particular college. On pages 53–56 you'll find brief explanations of the various checklist features; in Chapter 4 you'll find guidelines for using those features.

There are no uniform formats for college home pages, so colleges will differ in how they list and hyperlink topics. Focus on content rather than titles to gather the facts you want.

When you're ready to explore further, you'll find a wealth of information about the college, its admission and financial aid policies, academic programs, student services, and much more. Use Section II of the World Wide Web worksheet to record important details for future reference.

Section III is a catch-all area in which to note items of interest and other resources that don't fit into standard categories but may be very useful to refer to at a later date.

Using the example of Syracuse University's Web site, your worksheet would look like the one on pages 49–50.

Dr. H's World Wide Web Worksheet

Name of college _Syracuse University_

I. General Information

• College Web Site Checklist

☑ Greeting
☑ What's new
☑ Index to Web site
☐ Registration/guest book
☑ Directory
☑ Evaluation/feedback

☑ About the college
☑ Viewbook
☑ Campus tour
☐ College video
☑ Local events

☑ Upcoming events

☑ Admission information
☐ Financial aid information
☐ College application

☑ Academic departments
☐ Class schedule
☑ Campus policies
☑ Campus map

☑ Campus library
☐ Campus bookstore

☑ Student services
☐ Student organizations
☐ Student newspaper
☑ Personal home pages

☑ Faculty news
☐ Faculty newspaper
☑ Alumni information

II. Specific Information

• About the College

Location _small city, Upstate New York_ Enrollment size _10,000 full-time undergraduate, 4,500 graduate_

Type of college (public/private, etc.) _4-year private university, coed_

Make up of student body _from 50 states & 100+ countries, 18% minority background, average age 18_

Degrees offered _BA, BS, BFA, Barch, MA, MS, MBA, MFA, MSW, PhD, EdD, JD_

On-campus housing _11 residence halls_ Guaranteed for first year? _yes_ 4 years? _yes_

Percent of students living on campus _75% of all students_

Campus calendar (semester, quarter, trimester, 4-1-4) _semester_

Library facilities _more than 2.7 million volumes and over 3 million microforms_

• About Admission

Test requirements: SAT I _preferred_ SAT II _____ ACT _accepted_

Selection criteria (minimum test scores, GPA, essay, interview, etc.) _not available online; check The College Handbook or undergraduate admission office_

Percent of applicants accepted _n/a online_

Required high school preparation _n/a online_

Application deadlines: Early decision _11/15_ Regular _2/1_

Notification dates: Early decision _1/15_ Regular _3/15_

Candidate reply dates: Early decision _2/15_ Regular _5/1_

Continued on next page

• About Costs and Financial Aid

Tuition $16,710_____ Housing $3,920_____ Meals $3,520_____ Fees $370_____

Books and supplies $820_____ Other expenses n/a online Total $25,340_____

Type and % of financial aid awarded: Grants n/a_____ Loans n/a_____ Work n/a_____

Forms required FAFSA, for additional info go to_____

   http://sumweb.syr.edu/summon3/bulkdist/public/web/apply.htm_____

Application deadlines 2/15 for FAFSA_____

• About Academics

Range of courses in desired major see online listing_____

Student-faculty ratio 11:1 overall_____

Advanced Placement policy: Credit n/a, contact dept. Placement n/a, contact dept.

CLEP policy: Credit ditto AP_____ Placement ditto AP_____

Academic programs: Co-op education _____ Double major _____ Honors _____

  Internships _____ Student-designed major _____ Weekend college _____

  Cross-registration _____ Study abroad _____ Visiting/exchange student _____

  Washington semester _____ Other _____

_____

Graduation requirements_____

• About Student Life & Services

Services: Tutoring _____ Study skills/time management _____

  Freshman orientation _____

Career counseling _____ Health services _____

  Employment services for undergrads _____

Other_____

Athletics: Intramural many, check further for specifics_____

Intercollegiate ditto Intramural_____

Clubs ditto Intramural_____

Sororities/Fraternities 30 fraternities, 17 sororities_____

III. Comments, Special Features, Off-Site Resources

_____

_____

_____

_____

_____

_____

_____

Dr. H's World Wide Web Worksheet

Name of college _____

I. General Information

• College Web Site Checklist

- ❏ Greeting
- ❏ What's new
- ❏ Index to Web site
- ❏ Registration/Guest book
- ❏ Directory
- ❏ Evaluation/feedback

- ❏ About the college
- ❏ Viewbook
- ❏ Campus tour
- ❏ College video
- ❏ Local events

- ❏ Upcoming events
- ❏ Admission information
- ❏ Financial aid information
- ❏ College application
- ❏ Academic departments
- ❏ Class schedule
- ❏ Campus policies
- ❏ Campus map

- ❏ Campus library
- ❏ Campus bookstore
- ❏ Student services
- ❏ Student organizations
- ❏ Student newspaper
- ❏ Personal home pages
- ❏ Faculty news
- ❏ Faculty newspaper
- ❏ Alumni information

II. Specific Information

• About the College

Location _____ Enrollment size _____

_____

Type of college (public/private, etc.)_____

Make up of student body _____

_____

Degrees offered _____

On-campus housing _____ Guaranteed for first year? _____ 4 years? _____

Percent of students living on campus _____

Campus calendar (semester, quarter, trimester, 4-1-4) _____

Library facilities _____

• About Admission

Test requirements: SAT I_____ SAT II _____ ACT_____

Selection criteria (minimum test scores, GPA, essay, interview, etc.) _____

_____

Percent of applicants accepted _____

Required high school preparation _____

Application deadlines: Early decision _____ Regular _____

Notification dates: Early decision _____ Regular _____

Candidate reply dates: Early decision _____ Regular _____

Continued on next page

• About Costs and Financial Aid

Tuition _____ Housing _____ Meals _____ Fees _____

Books and supplies _____ Other expenses _____ Total _____

Type and % of financial aid awarded: Grants _____ Loans _____ Work _____

Forms required _____

_____

Application deadlines _____

• About Academics

Range of courses in desired major _____

Student-faculty ratio_____

Advanced Placement policy: Credit _____ Placement _____

CLEP policy: Credit _____ Placement _____

Academic programs: Co-op education _____ Double major _____ Honors _____

  Internships _____ Student-designed major _____ Weekend college _____

  Cross-registration _____ Study abroad _____ Visiting/exchange student _____

  Washington semester _____ Other _____

_____

Graduation requirements _____

• About Student Life & Services

Services: Tutoring _____ Study skills/time management _____

  Freshman orientation _____

Career counseling _____ Health services _____

  Employment services for undergrads _____

Other_____

Athletics: Intramural _____

Intercollegiate _____

Clubs _____

Sororities/Fraternities_____

III. Comments, Special Features, Off-Site Resources

_____

_____

_____

_____

_____

_____

Checklist Definitions

About the college: gives facts and figures, such as size of student body, date the college was founded, number of buildings, campus acreage, names of famous alumni, etc.

Academic departments: the place to look for specific information about an academic area that interests you; often includes e-mail addresses of faculty and current students.

Admission information: often another name for "News for New Students," giving information about the college aimed at prospective applicants; usually includes an admission application as well.

Alumni information: the Web site area to visit for facts about graduates of a particular college—often found under listing for the Office of Alumni Affairs.

Campus bookstore: the college's Web site for buying books, sweatshirts, banners, and other rah-rah stuff.

Campus library: the site for finding out about the quality of the college's library.

Campus map/location: some sites include an actual map of the campus and surrounding area.

Campus policies and procedures: the area that contains information about academic rules and student conduct.

Campus tour: gives you a look at the campus via pictures or video.

Class schedule: the Web site area that lists courses being offered during the year, with the name of the instructor and, in some instances, maximum class size.

College application: an electronic version that permits you to submit your application online.

College video: this is sometimes part of the viewbook Web site; note that it often takes a long time to download and requires special software to view in full motion.

Directory (sometimes called "white pages"): the Web location that contains the names, titles, and office, home, and e-mail addresses of students, faculty, staff, and alumni.

Evaluation/feedback form: your chance to give the college your comments on its Web site.

Faculty News: usually lists academic resources, both on and off campus, including new academic newsgroups and online scholarly journals.

Faculty/staff newspaper: an official publication of the college to showcase important events and accomplishments.

Financial aid information: where to look for facts about a college's financial aid policies, including application deadlines and tips on applying for financial aid (see Chapter 6 for more information about financial aid).

Greeting: this area may be a video, audio, or text message from the college's president or other senior official.

Index of Web site: lets you search the site using key words, e.g., "directory."

Local events information: gives details about cultural, social, and recreational opportunities around the campus. Look for links to local newspapers, chamber of commerce, government offices, and community groups.

News for new students: often the site where information from the admission office is posted.

Personal home page: the Web location where staff, students, and alumni can post their opinions and advice, free of official restrictions.

Registration form/guest book: lets a college know who you are and that you've visited its Web site, if you choose to sign in.

Student groups and organizations: a listing of all academic and social groups sanctioned by the college.

Student newspaper: an unofficial source of information about campus life from the students' point of view, generally independent of the college and sometimes in disagreement with the administration.

Student services: here's where you'll find information about non-academic departments, like housing, career planning, dean of students, and financial aid.

Upcoming events: dates, times, and descriptions of on-campus activities (open houses, concerts, lectures) can be found here.

Viewbook: an electronic version of the facts, figures, and pictures published in the college's printed viewbook.

What's new: the area updated most frequently, alerting users about new areas on the college's Web site and/or upcoming events on campus.

Chapter 4

E-Mail— Communicating with the World on the Web

Building Your Information Network on the Web

Signing on to the Internet gives you virtually instant access to anyone with an e-mail address. When you're gathering college information, that can be a great advantage because it enables you to contact a wide range of people who have facts, opinions, and advice about colleges you want to know more about.

Before the Internet existed, your research possibilities were fairly limited. You might have an interview with someone in the admission office and talk with a few enrolled students and faculty while visiting a campus. Or someone in your

58 family, or a friend or two, might have known enough about a particular college to give you a broader perspective—though not necessarily very current information.

Now, by turning on your computer and signing on to the Internet, you can get in touch with dozens of enrolled students, faculty, student services administrators, and alumni to get answers to just about any question you might have, including:

- pros and cons of taking a double major
- availability of internships
- possibilities for off-campus jobs to help you stretch your budget
- campus security measures
- quality of student health services
- access to special programs for overcoming a learning disability

The only limits to researching colleges via the Internet are your own interests and tenacity.

Launching Your E-Mail Campaign

Your campaign starts at the college's Web site, where you'll gather names and e-mail addresses. Some colleges have a directory on the home page, so this information is easy to find. Other colleges make you search a little further, using an index and key word. Some colleges post their e-mail addresses by department or administrative office. For students' e-mail addresses, be sure to check the listings for student groups and clubs. Many of the major search sites are now indexing college sites, making it easy to find and link to a college's e-mail directory. Check out the following:

http://Yahoo.com/education/university/indices

This might be a good time to take a second look at the list of Net Facts in Chapter 1—particularly the one about the relationship between persistence and rewards, on page 4. Keep in mind that 8 out of 10 colleges provide students, faculty, and staff with e-mail addresses, so you're likely to find a lot of well-informed people ready to help you. Temple University in Philadelphia, for example, reports having more than 60,000 e-mail accounts (students, faculty, administrators).

Some college Web sites provide a directory of names without e-mail addresses, but you can usually construct the address yourself by keying in the person's first initial and last name, followed by @, followed by the name of the college, followed by "edu." For example: jsmith@collegename .edu. If that method doesn't work, contact the admission office by e-mail to ask for the correct domain.

Access for High School Students

A growing number of colleges provide you with a personal e-mail address and free access to the campus computer once you've been offered admission, even though you're still in high school. Imagine the facts and insights you can gain from e-mail exchanges with your future classmates and mentors!

Important Next Steps

Once you have the names and e-mail addresses of people at the colleges you're interested in, it's time to get in touch. There are at least five groups or individuals that you'll want to contact since each offers a different perspective on the college:

- admission director
- enrolled students
- faculty
- alumni
- financial aid director

Use the E-mail Log on page 66 to keep track of your contacts. It's a useful summary for quick reference in the future.

You'll find all or most of the basic information about a college on its Web site—facts ranging from application deadlines and fees, costs, statistics on last year's freshman class, and a lot of details about student life. If your college Web site searches don't turn up that kind of information or answers to questions such as the following ones, it's time to send e-mail to administrators, students, faculty, and alumni.

- What percentage of Early Decision applicants were accepted last year?
- What kind of internship and placement services are available? Are companies encouraged to visit the col-

lege for recruiting purposes?

- What percentage of freshmen return as sophomores?
- What percentage of entering students graduate in four years? In five years?
- What percentage of last year's graduating class went on to graduate school?
- Are computers widely available to students? Can the system be accessed from dorm rooms?

Here are sample e-mail messages that you can adapt to your own writing style and interests to gather more information. For a sample message to financial aid officers, see Chapter 6.

Sample E-Mail Message to Director of Admission

TO: admissiondirectorname@collegename.edu
FROM: yourname@xxx.com
Subject: Can You Help Me?

Message:

Hi. I'm seriously considering applying to your institution. Could you or someone on your staff please take a few minutes to give me the following information?

Is it possible to get the e-mail addresses of several students majoring in (subject you're interested in) who might be willing to answer a few of my questions?

I'd also like to have the e-mail addresses of several students who graduated from my high school who might be willing to answer my questions.

Thank you for taking the time to respond.

your name
high school name
home phone number
(if you'd like to be contacted by phone)

Sample E-Mail Message to Enrolled Students

TO: studentname@collegename.edu
FROM: yourname@xxx.com
Subject: Can You Help Me?

....

Message:

Hi. I'm seriously considering applying to your college and majoring in (subject you're interested in). I'd appreciate it if you could answer any or all of the following questions and forward this message to anyone else whose comments you think would be helpful.

1. What year are you in, and how would you describe your instructors? Are they accessible? Do most of them know you by name?

2. What was the average number of students in your freshman-year courses? Were they taught by professors or teaching assistants?

3. How would you describe the "typical" student at your college? Have any of your friends transferred to other colleges? If so, why?

4. How would you rate student services, such as counseling, campus security, etc.?

5. How would you rate the college's academic advising system?

6. Are you getting any financial aid from the college? Is the financial aid office helpful?

7. If you had to do it over again, would you have chosen the same college?

Many thanks for taking the time to answer my questions.

your name
high school name
home phone number
(if you'd like to be contacted by phone)

Sample E-Mail Message to Faculty

TO: facultyname@collegename.edu
FROM: yourname@xxx.com
Subject: Can You Help Me?

Message:

Hi. I'm seriously considering applying to your college to major in (subject that interests you) and would like to know more about the faculty. I hope you can spare the time to answer some or all of the following questions:

1. Do you prefer teaching or research? Do schedules and facilities give you a chance to do both? Do freshmen ever have a chance to take courses with senior faculty members?

2. What do you consider the greatest rewards and challenges in working with students?

3. Would you please give me information about one or two of your publications so that I can read them. Are you active in any scholarly associations in your field?

4. What are your research and/or teaching interests? Do you and your colleagues involve undergraduate students in research projects? Are there paid research assistant positions open to juniors or seniors?

5. Is there much turnover in your department? What percentage of the faculty in your department is fulltime? What role do graduate students play in undergraduate teaching?

I'd appreciate it if you could forward this message to any other faculty who might be willing to answer my questions.

Many thanks for your time and help.

your name
high school name
home phone number
(if you'd like to be contacted by phone)

Sample E-Mail Message to Alumni

TO: alumnusname@collegename.edu
FROM: yourname@xxx.com
Subject: Can You Help Me?

Message:

Hi. I'm seriously considering applying to your alma mater and would appreciate your comments on your undergraduate experience there. Would you please take a few moments to respond to the following questions:

1. How would you characterize the "typical" student at (name) College?

2. What is your overall opinion of the faculty? Accessible? Interested in teaching undergraduates?

3. Did the college help you with your postgraduate plans? Did the college provide the background you needed in your major? Did you find a job in your field soon after graduation? Are you working in your field now and pleased with it?

4. Do you feel that being an alumnus of your institution is an asset in your profession?

5. If you continued your education after graduation, did the college provide good preparation for graduate school? Was your college's reputation a help in gaining acceptance to the graduate school of your choice?

6. What were the best and worst aspects of your undergraduate years at the college? What would you change about the college if you could?

7. Finally, if you had to do it over again, would you attend the same or a different college?

Thank you for taking the time to respond.

your name
high school name
home phone number
(if you'd like to be contacted by phone)

E-Mail Log

Name of College _____

Name of Administrator	Date Sent	Date Received	Comments
_____	_____	_____	_____
_____	_____	_____	_____
_____	_____	_____	_____
_____	_____	_____	_____

Name of Student	Date Sent	Date Received	Comments
_____	_____	_____	_____
_____	_____	_____	_____
_____	_____	_____	_____
_____	_____	_____	_____

Name of Faculty	Date Sent	Date Received	Comments
_____	_____	_____	_____
_____	_____	_____	_____
_____	_____	_____	_____
_____	_____	_____	_____

Name of Alumnus	Date Sent	Date Received	Comments
_____	_____	_____	_____
_____	_____	_____	_____
_____	_____	_____	_____
_____	_____	_____	_____

_____
_____
_____

Make as many photocopies of the blank log sheet as you need. Or, if you want to maintain your records electronically, set up a similar form on your computer.

Chapter 5

Other College Web Sites to Check Out

Personal Home Pages

At many colleges, faculty, staff, students, and alumni have personal home pages (PHPs for short), which offer unique perspectives on the particular institution and the people associated with it. Each of these unofficial sites is likely to have a different agenda and purpose. By exploring them, you can often pick up a lot of valuable information that doesn't find its way into viewbooks or college catalogs, such as:

- students' opinions about the college's academic programs
- student–faculty relationships

- the intellectual, social, political, and cultural climate at that college
- problem areas, controversies, and much more

Let's take a look at what you might find on the various types of PHPs.

Faculty PHPs

Faculty PHPs typically focus on academic and scholarly information about the person's teaching and research interests, class schedules, professional accomplishments, and recent publications. Some include a professional resume or curriculum vitae. When you're visiting faculty PHPs, it's a good idea to note and record on your Web worksheet the individual's accomplishments, e-mail address, and any other facts or figures that seem pertinent.

You'll find that home pages, including faculty PHPs, will hyperlink you to their favorite Web sites and sometimes to areas of personal talents, hobbies, and skills, as well as professional interests, such as the home page for the American Biological Association or the home page for the American Civil Liberties Union. You might want to surf a few of their hyperlinks to see if they offer any pertinent information or insights. For example, you might find a link to the American Biological Association's Web site that includes a valuable listserv and/or newsgroup where you can ask people in the field for their recommendations on colleges they think have particularly strong biology departments.

Students, Alumni, Faculty & Staff Web Pages

The contents and views expressed in these pages are not necessarily those of The College of New Jersey.

This page is automatically updated at certain times during the day. The next scheduled update of this page is at

PM

If you just created your web home page, you must wait until the time above for it to show up on this list. You **do not** have to manually register it. The system will find your index.html file in your www directory and put it in the list.

Search Home pages (**index.html**)

Select this line if your browser does not support tables (like *Lynx*, *CMS WWW* and *Netscape* before version 1.1).

If the text below is garbled, click here.

[Faculty & Staff | Students | Alumni]

Faculty & Staff	*Accounts are alphabetized by login name*		
Richard Albe	Judith A. Alu	Glenda Alvin	Norman L Asper
William Ball	Pete Benken	Robert Bittner	Renae Bredin
James Bricker	Cloe Collura	Timothy Chang	Ed Conjura
Ching-Tai Shih	Gloria H Dickinson	Anne Disdier	Ralph Edelbach
George Facas	Larry Furman	Ron Gleeson	Anne Gormly
Jean E Graham	Tod H. Herring	Harry Hess	James Chianese
Joseph F. Flynn	Joseph Lopez	Jeff Kerswill	Deborah Knox
Leon Brooks	Donald Leake	David W. Letcher	Timothy C. McGee
Michael Mensch	Mort Winston	Norm Neff	Romulo Ochoa
Kathy Oliver	H. C. Rawicz	John S Riddle	Robert A. Maarberg
Rosanne Meister	Francis A Romano	Ruane Miller	Philip Sanders
Shou Rei Chang	Shawn Sivy	Brad Stober	Tim S. Smith
Chamont Wang	Edward Watson	Michael Wodynski	Ursula Wolz
Dr R Donald Wright	Yahudah Fowler	Gregg Ziliani	

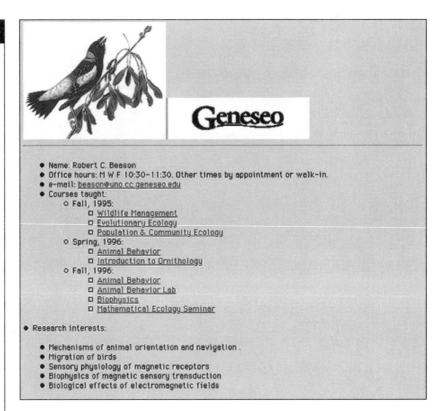

- Name: Robert C. Beason
- Office hours: M W F 10:30-11:30. Other times by appointment or walk-in.
- e-mail: beason@uno.cc.geneseo.edu
- Courses taught:
    - Fall, 1995:
        - Wildlife Management
        - Evolutionary Ecology
        - Population & Community Ecology
    - Spring, 1996:
        - Animal Behavior
        - Introduction to Ornithology
    - Fall, 1996:
        - Animal Behavior
        - Animal Behavior Lab
        - Biophysics
        - Mathematical Ecology Seminar

- Research interests:

    - Mechanisms of animal orientation and navigation .
    - Migration of birds
    - Sensory physiology of magnetic receptors
    - Biophysics of magnetic sensory transduction
    - Biological effects of electromagnetic fields

Some faculty members will put information about their courses on their PHP. Reading a course syllabus, test schedule, and term paper requirements can give you a sense of how challenging, comprehensive, and current the course, curriculum, and instructor might be.

Staff PHPs

Staff PHPs typically provide more official than unofficial information. But, like faculty, administrative staff often include their professional background and links to other Web

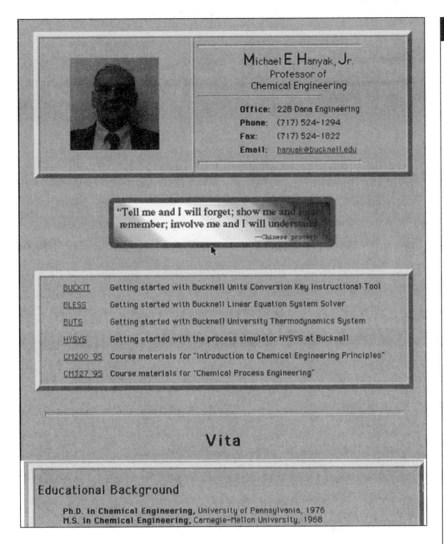

sites they think are of interest. For example, a director of admission might link you to informal chat rooms that focus on college admission issues that could give you some useful insights. Or a financial aid officer might link you to a Web site that provides information on scholarships and low-interest loans.

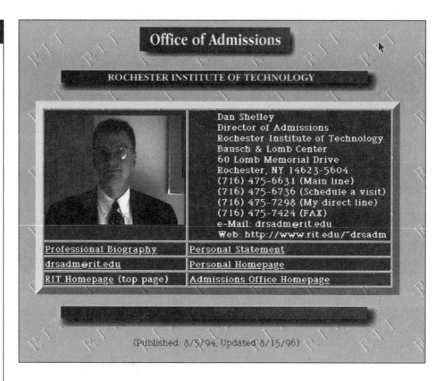

Dan Shelley
Director of Admissions
Rochester Institute of Technology
Bausch & Lomb Center
60 Lomb Memorial Drive
Rochester, NY 14623-5604
(716) 475-6631 (Main line)
(716) 475-6736 (Schedule a visit)
(716) 475-7298 (My direct line)
(716) 475-7424 (FAX)
e-Mail: drsadm@rit.edu
Web: http://www.rit.edu/~drsadm

Professional Biography	Personal Statement
drsadm@rit.edu	Personal Homepage
RIT Homepage (top page)	Admissions Office Homepage

(Published: 8/5/94, Updated 8/15/96)

Student PHPs

Student PHPs can be a lively source of unofficial, often irreverent, information about a college. Some are likely to lead you to a lot of good insights and advice. Some will give you a vivid sense of the campus climate. Others may seem silly, nerdy, or just a waste of time. They are highly subjective, usually uncensored by the college, and sometimes contain language and links that may be offensive to you, but the option of staying or leaving is always yours. That's one of the key aspects of exploring the Web. You're in control of where and how you spend time on the Web and what you get from it.

When you're surfing student PHPs, it's a good idea to keep
a record of pertinent information and reactions on your
Web worksheet. Pay particular attention to other students'
favorite Web sites, which may hyperlink you
to helpful sources of information—both on and off
campus.

Alumni PHPs

Alumni PHPs can be particularly useful in giving you
insight into the potential practical value of your tuition
investment. In other words, by browsing alumni sites you
can infer a lot about how effectively a college prepares its
graduates for their postgraduation goals—whether they're
heading for graduate school or the world of work. Are
alumni generally enthusiastic about their undergraduate
experience—teaching staff, the quality of the courses they
were offered, their relationships with professors and
administrative staff as well as with fellow students? Are
they involved now in interesting, challenging jobs and pro-
fessions? Do they seem to maintain close ties with the college? Those are all clues to aspects of a college that may
not surface in your other investigations.

If alums put a phone number on their PHP, you can assume
they don't mind getting phone calls, but e-mail is probably
the better way to contact them with questions. Again, be
sure to keep a record on your Web worksheet of all pertinent
information you gather from this important source.

!!WELCOME!!

After being on the internet for two years (and procrastinating for about 11 months) this homepage has finally come into existence. Contained within are little bits and pieces of what makes me

ME.

For starters, I am a senior at the

University of Pennsylvania IN The Wharton School

My twin majors are Entrepreneurial Management and Management Information Systems. I have held a workstudy position for two and a half years at

as the Student Manager of the Video Bulletin Board, ResNet Channel 2.

Notice: This site is designed to work with Netscape Navigator. Other browsers may not display properly. (I have tested the AOL browser and it does not display correctly)

In March of 1995, I decided to get serious with my graphic design work, so I formed a company, Singularity Design, Inc. Since that time, Singularity has done work for two of the four undergraduate colleges at Penn (Wharton, SEAS), local magazines, Philadelphia's largest information provider, LibertyNet, and the School District of Philadelphia (starting August 15).

 Corporate Website

 My Personal Philosophy

At the start of 1996, more than 400 colleges had online versions of their student-run newspapers on the Web, and predictions are that virtually all student newspapers will be online by the end of the decade. They're a great source of unofficial information because they express the ideas, interests, and opinions of the students themselves and give you a real feel for what's happening on campus.

Many online campus newspapers include a search feature that lets you use key words to quickly find articles on topics of special interest to you. For example, if you searched the University of Pennsylvania's student-run newspaper (*The Daily Pennsylvanian*, http://www.dp.upenn.edu) using the key words "crime on campus," you'd get the full text of the whole range of articles and op-ed pieces on that topic that appeared in past editions of the paper. With Web access, you no longer have to rely on one or two issues of the paper that you might have seen when you visited the campus to keep you in touch with what's happening at a college you're interested in attending.

Faculty Newspapers and Other Publications

Faculty newspapers, bulletins, and magazines are produced by the college administration to keep the campus community informed about what's happening at the college. In them you will often see listings and reports about the accomplish-

The Michigan Daily Online

Back issues of the Michigan Daily Online

August 1996

	August 14, 1996	August 7, 1996

July 1996

July 31, 1996	July 24, 1996	
July 17, 1996	July 10, 1996	July 3, 1996

June 1996

June 19, 1996	June 12, 1996	June 5, 1996

May 1996

May 29, 1996		
May 22, 1996	May 15, 1996	May 8, 1996

Winter 1996: January 10 through April 23, 1996

1995: May 3 through December 10, 1995

©1996 The Michigan Daily

Letters to the editor should be sent to
online.daily@umich.edu

Other College Web Sites to Check Out

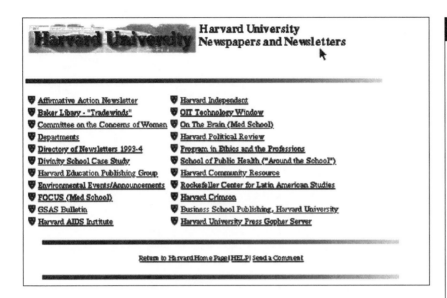

ments of faculty and senior administrators, such as recent publications, grants received, honors awarded, service performed, speeches given. They're good sources to explore periodically for that sort of official information.

Alumni Information

The information on these Web pages is usually about upcoming alumni events, but some colleges post alumni e-mail addresses, newsgroups, and the home and office addresses of their graduates. Alumni voluntarily provide the information, knowing that it's available to anyone who wants to contact them, so you needn't be shy about doing so.

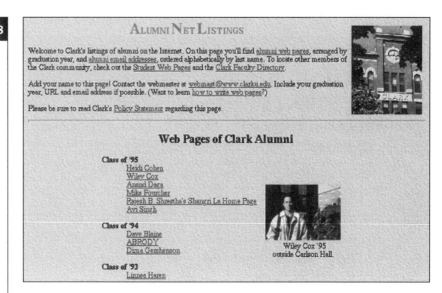

Student Groups and Organizations

Click your mouse here and you're likely to see listings and hyperlinks to dozens of student-run organizations on and off campus. The following are just a few of the kinds of sites to expect:

- Biology Club
- Student Government
- Commuter Students Association
- Minority Student Union
- In-line Skaters Online

As you browse the home pages of groups that sound interesting to you, pay particular attention to the types of activities being sponsored, the extent of student participation, minutes of meetings, e-mail addresses of student leaders, and any

World Alumni Net

- Asia
  - China
  - Hong Kong
  - India
  - Indonesia
  - Korea
  - Philippines
  - Taiwan
  - Singapore
- Australia
- Europe
  - Poland
  - United Kingdom
- North America
  - Canada
    - British Columbia
    - Ontario
  - U.S.A.
    - Alabama
    - Arizona
    - California
      - Northern California
      - Southern California
    - Connecticut
    - Florida
    - Georgia
    - Idaho
    - Illinois
    - Iowa
    - Kentucky
    - Louisiana
    - Maryland
    - Massachusetts
    - Michigan
    - Minnesota
    - Missouri
    - Nebraska
    - New York
    - North Carolina
    - Ohio
    - Oklahoma
    - Oregon
    - Pennsylvania
    - South Carolina
    - Tennessee
    - Texas
    - Utah
    - Washington

To add a new area, click here.
For comments and/or suggestions, please send e-mail to alumni@infophil.com.

Student Organization Directory

Welcome to the Student Organization Directory at Cornell University.

All organizations are required to register with the Student Activities Office each fall. Deadline for the 1996-97 academic year is Wednesday September 4. This file will be updated with the following information for each organization as they register: Name of organization; Description; Address; Phone; Web site; Contact person; Advisor information.

Please join us September 9-13, 11:00 a.m.-2:00 p.m. in the Willard Straight Hall Memorial Room for the Annual Student Activities Fair. Different organizations are represented each day. Come and GET INVOLVED!

Organizations may now have access to FREE space on the internet for an organization homepage. Please contact the Office of the University Registrar (255-4232) or the Assistant Director of Student Activities (255-4169) for information.

For further information on student organizations or events, please contact the Student Activities Office at 255-4169 or visit us on the fifth floor of Willard Straight Hall.

A **CU***info* PAGE

linkages to other off-campus Web sites. For instance, the Student Marketing Club might have a hyperlink to the American Marketing Association's home page, where additional resources and information can be found.

Academic Information and/or Departments

This area of a college's Web site is an electronic version of the college catalog, filled with essential information about academic offerings and requirements. You're likely to find hyperlinks to:

- all academic departments
- course descriptions
- test date calendar for the year
- home pages for specific courses
- policies, procedures, and much more

After a quick overall look to get a general idea of what's available, go back to the start of the area and hyperlink to an academic department that interests you to get more detailed facts about:

- required and elective courses with instructors' names
- departmental faculty directory, often including e-mail addresses and hyperlinks to personal home pages
- bulletin board service for some courses

Your task is to look for answers to the two critically important questions listed below.

1. To what extent are tenured professors, rather than part-time instructors or graduate students, teaching freshman-level courses?

Steps to follow:

- read the course descriptions
- find and record the names of 10 entry-level courses
- find the list of courses being offered in the spring and/or fall semester
- record the name of the instructor assigned to each course
- search the faculty/staff directory to find out the instructor's rank and employment status
- record your findings on your Web worksheet

2. How challenging are the courses and will I be able to keep up with my classmates?

Steps to follow:

- search for course home pages
- read the course syllabus (if a syllabus isn't provided online, e-mail the instructor or department chair to ask that one be mailed to your home address)
- browse through the assignments and examination schedule
- read some of the student papers/reports that are online to get a sense of the level at which other students are working

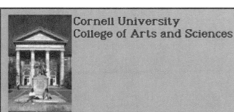

Cornell University
College of Arts and Sciences

Department of Asian Studies

- ## About the Department of Asian Studies

  Contacting the department; who's who in the department

- ## Faculty Information

  Faculty directory

- ## Academic Information

  Course Descriptions; Course Schedules (Fa 96)

  Course Schedules (Sp 96); Final Exam info (Sp 96)

  Academic Calendar; Courses of Study

Also see Asian Studies courses listed under Agricultural Economics,
Anthropology, Asian-American, Art History, Architecture, Communications,
Languages, Linguistics, Economics, Government, History, ILR, Music,
Rural Sociology, Sociology, and Society/Humanities.

- ## The Undergraduate Major

  Honors Work; Intensive Language Program (FALCON); Study Abroad

Information for New/ Prospective Students/ Admission Information

As you might expect, this area of a college's Web site is designed to recruit new students and encourage them to apply. It generally contains a lot of good, official information and often includes an online admission application.

This is where you'll find:

- facts and figures about the college
- a multimedia presentation highlighting the institution's best features
- student testimonials about what a great place it is
- faculty profiles and statistics
- a campus map and directions for getting to the campus
- basic admission information (deadlines, academic requirements, times for campus tours, degrees offered, a profile of last year's entering class, an online form for requesting a catalog, etc.)

Some colleges provide a BBS and/or a listserv for new students, while others encourage you to e-mail the office with questions. Be sure to register for any online service made available by the admission office.

Other College Web Sites to Check Out

Faculty Titles in Order of Seniority and Experience

Full Professor: almost always a tenured position, normally appointed after 10–15 years' experience, demonstrated accomplishment, Ph.D.

Associate Professor: usually a tenured position, normally appointed after 5–10 years' experience, with same basic qualifications as full professor

Assistant Professor: often an entry-level position with the potential for tenure

Instructor: typically a person who has not yet earned an advanced academic degree, may teach full- or part-time

Adjunct: always a temporary position with no long-term commitment from the college or the employee; depending on professional experience and academic degrees, may be appointed as adjunct professor, adjunct associate professor, adjunct assistant professor, or adjunct instructor

Graduate Assistant: graduate students teaching undergraduate courses under the supervision of a professor

Off-Campus Web Sites

There are hundreds of Web sites that offer you wonderful information about a college and/or a particular aspect of the college but have no official connection with the institution. A few of them are listed in Appendix E, and home pages for some of them appear on pages 86-91.

BLACK EXCEL: THE COLLEGE HELP NETWORK

Help with College Selection, Admission, Scholarships and Aid

What Is BLACK EXCEL?

BLACK EXCEL is a college admissions and scholarship service for African-American students. Since its founding in 1988 by Isaac J. Black, BLACK EXCEL has helped young people and their parents all across the country to navigate the difficult college admission process. We have tried to make the way easy and accessible. As a result, we are happy to say that we have helped hundreds of African Americans get into college who might otherwise not have done so.

Students we have counseled have gained entry to over a hundred different colleges, including both Historically Black and mainstream institutions. The list comprises an "honor roll" of schools, touching every level of excellence and entrance difficulty. Whether a student was looking to Spelman, Yale, Hampton, Boston College or a lesser known school, we knew how to help. As a result, scores of our children are now looking to brighter futures. Some are already in law, medical and graduate schools.

Right from the beginning, parents asked us for scholarship help. Nearly all were concerned about how to finance their children's higher education. BLACK EXCEL got busy creating our first Scholarship List. Not only did students and parents request the List. Libraries, colleges, high schools, churches, and other organizations did so as well. Write-ups about BLACK EXCEL began to appear in *Black Collegian, Career Focus, College Preview,* and other magazines and newspapers. Our list was called "the most comprehensive" available for Black students. Last year, Gail Ann Schlachter, editor of *A Guide for Minority Scholarships* decided to use BLACK EXCEL as a key source of scholarship information in the new edition of her highly respected book.

BLACK EXCEL services have expanded over the years to include an updated, 350+ Scholarship List; a personalized College Help Package; a quarterly newsletter; a reference guide to 143 Historically Black Colleges, detailed profiles of individual schools (to read BLACK EXCEL's profile of Morgan State, click here); and a Medical School Help Package. For more information and a free copy of BLACK EXCEL's newsletter, e-mail jjblack@cnct.com

You can read an article by I.J. Black, "Blacks and Those 'Gold Card' Tests" by clicking here.

The Black Excel QUICK REFERENCE GUIDE TO HISTORICALLY BLACK COLLEGES (including BLACK EXCEL'S TOP 10): Profiles, SAT scores, alumni associations and contact people .

For a menu of BLACK EXCEL products and services, click here.

Or write to:

BLACK EXCEL
28 Vesey Street
Suite 2239
New York, NY 10007

Or call:
(718) 527-8896

The Best of African-American Cyberspace

Historically Black Colleges (Special Programs & Majors, Greeks and more)

Historically Black Colleges & Universities Graduate Fellowship Program (for those interested in science and engineering)

Newsgroups

Many, if not all, of the commerical online services provide subscribers with a forum—typically, a bulletin board—for discussing college admission and financial aid issues and concerns. For example:

America Online offers a bulletin board where you can post questions and comments to an experienced counselor who responds regularly with information and advice on all aspects of choosing and applying to college. The bulletin board also serves as a forum for exchanging information with other AOL users. Another option AOL offers users is the ability to browse and word search the entire text of *The College Handbook* for in-depth college information about all accredited two-year and four-year colleges. Go to the Learning and

HILLEL

Click on the images below for information

General Information

the X-CHANGE
HILLEL'S PROGRAM RESOURCE EXCHANGE

Student Services

Campus Profiles

Hillel Publications

Other College Web Sites to Check Out

COLLEGE FAIR

- School Rankings
- Colleges & Universities
- Graduate Schools
- Financial Aid
- Career Files
- College Fair Infobank
- This Week's Issue

OUTLOOK
COLUMNISTS
U.S. NEWS
WORLD REPORT
BUSINESS & TECH
CULTURE & IDEAS
NEWS YOU CAN USE

H I G H L I G H T S

▶ GRADUATE SCHOOLS

Journalism Grad Schools

Is going to J-school the way to land a job?

▶ TECHNOLOGY

Applying Online

How to connect to a school via the Web

EXTRA, EXTRA:

GRADUATE SCHOOLS: Supreme Court Lets Ruling Stand That Threatens Affirmative Action
COLLEGES: VMI must open its doors to women
CATALOG: All new, 1996 America's Best Graduate Schools guidebook from U.S. News

FREE! YOUR OWN HOME PAGE

CORPORATE LINKS

MAIN MENU | SEARCH | NEWS WATCH | WASHINGTON CONNECTION | NEWS YOU CAN USE | COLLEGE FAIR | TOWN HALL | ISSUE

HOT! HOT! HOT!
Just released -- the 1996 U.S. News America's Best Graduate Schools guidebook, only from U.S. News. Get the exclusive rankings. Plus, get the latest on admissions, financial aid, job prospects and more! Order yours now from the Catalog.

US NEWS CATALOG
Check out The U.S. News Catalog of Products. It's all here: exclusive U.S. News books, CD-Roms, and other exciting products! Find what you're looking for on colleges, graduate schools, hospitals, travel and more!

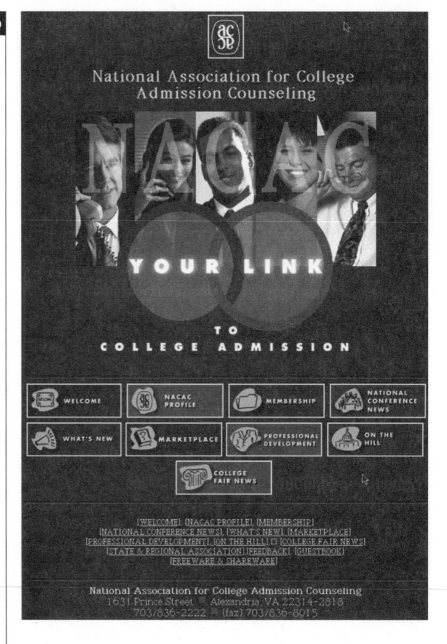

The On-Line Service Providing Information About
Institutional Capabilities of Historically
Black Colleges and Universities and
Hispanic-Serving Institutions

Academia

Federal Government

Access MOLIS via Internet or Modem

Minority On-Line Information System

User's Guide • July 1995 • Version 1.0 / Release 1.0

MOLIS can help you...

- **Identify research and educational capabilities**
  ...of Historically Black Colleges and Universities (HBCUs) and Hispanic-Serving Institutions (HSIs).

- **Contact the right people**
  ...within the minority education community.

- **Secure free computer and research equipment**
  ...for your school.

Reference department, and click on College Board Online to access these resources.

Prodigy lets you jump to "college bb" or browse a complete list of discussion items.

CompuServe offers access to Peterson's College Database, which contains information on 3,500 accredited colleges, as well as discussion groups (to access, use key word ed forum) on admission testing, campus life, and dorm living.

Joining a Newsgroup

New newsgroups that discuss college admissions and financial aid are springing up every day. Before long, you'll find thousands of different newsgroups for every college in the country and every facet of college life, including special newsgroups for parents of college-bound students and college counselors.

Interested in attending a state college in New Jersey? Soon you'll find a special newsgroup where students (high school and college) from around the world will be discussing the pros and cons of New Jersey's state colleges and universities.

Looking for creative ways to pay for a private college? Soon you'll find a special newsgroup where parents from around the nation will be discussing investment strategies, conversations they've had with financial aid directors at various institutions, and more.

Most newsgroups are unmoderated and open to the public. There are, however, a few unwritten rules and expectations when joining a newsgroup:

Look Before You Leap

Take the time to familiarize yourself with issues that have taken place in the group within the past 90 days. Loyal members of a newsgroup don't like having to respond to questions or issues already discussed. To catch up with the group, you'll want to read previously posted questions and responses (called message threads), then join the group with a question or comment.

Don't Be a Lurker

Once you have a good sense of the topics discussed, introduce yourself to the group by sending a message or posting a question. You might simply tell the members your reasons for joining the group and offer your help, when and if needed. Lurkers, those who only read messages and don't contribute to the group, are not demonstrating good Net etiquette.

Keep Current

As a member of any group, you need to keep current on what is being said and discussed by your fellow group members. Make a point of reading your newsgroup at least once a week.

You can find the most complete and updated list of Internet discussion groups at:

Deja News
http://www.dejanews.com

Listservs or Mailing Lists

Although still few in number, college-bound mailing lists on the Internet are increasing each month. By subscribing to a list, you're likely to receive dozens of e-mail messages each day from people asking for and sharing information on colleges. Some mailing lists are monitored (someone determines what is mailable) and some are unmonitored (anything goes). You can find the most complete and up-to-date list of Internet mailing lists at:

L-soft International
(http://www.lsoft.com/lists/listref.html)

L-Soft
international

CataList, the catalog of **LISTSERV** lists

Last update: 23 Aug 1996 (8,786 lists)

CataList
Reference site

Welcome to *CataList*, the catalog of LISTSERV lists! From this page, you can browse any of the 8,786 public LISTSERV lists on the Internet, search for mailing lists of interest, and get information about LISTSERV host sites. This information is generated automatically from LISTSERV's *LISTS database* and is always up to date.

List information

- Search for a mailing list of interest
- View lists by host site
- View lists by host country
- View lists with 10,000 subscribers or more
- View lists with 1,000 subscribers or more

Site information

- Search for a LISTSERV site of interest
- View sites in alphabetical order
- View sites by country

Information for list owners

- Provide HTML descriptions for your lists to enhance their appearance in the database.
- View or download the LISTSERV list owner's guide.

Internet Chat Rooms

Internet chat rooms (ICRs) provide a fast, direct, and lively way of getting information about a college. Simply "enter" the chat room (go to the site) and take part in whatever discussion is taking place at the time. You can find one of the best ICRs on college life (including admission) at:

> http://www.goodnet.com/%7Eroberte/
> webchatnavigator.html

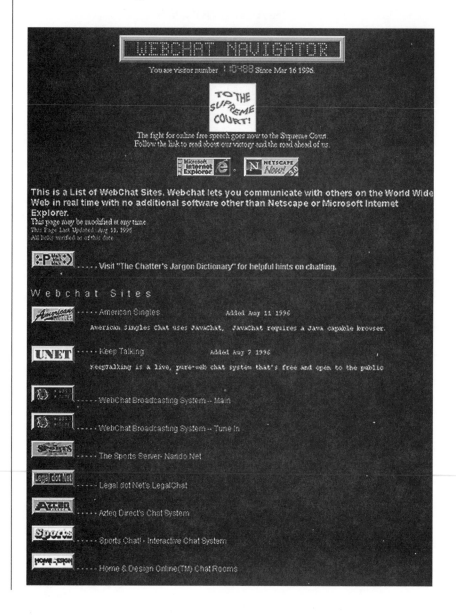

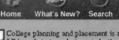

College Counseling

Home   What's New?   Search

College planning and placement is a major focus at LFA, and starts early in a student's career. Our College Counseling office works with students throughout their time at LFA, to give them the best possible chance of being accepted to the college of their choice.

At LFA, we know that the right school isn't always the biggest, or even the best-known school. We work hard to find the right school for each student's needs, interests, and abilities.

Our emphasis on excellence, preparation, and planning pays big dividends. One hundred percent of our graduates go on to college, and the list of colleges our students have been accepted to is impressive.

- College Acceptances for the Class of 1996
- College Acceptances for the Class of 1995
- Ask our Director of College Planning and Placement about college choices at LFA
- LFA's Academic Statistics

Outward Bound

Here are some links to places that LFA students, parents, and advisors may find useful.

College Information

- The College Prep Page lists over 100 Internet college resources to help you find a college, plan your career, get into college, get financial aid, and more. Very useful!
- CollegeNet
  An online source for information about institutions of higher education.

Testing, review courses, etc.

- Testprep has hit the web! If you would like to study for the SAT I, this is the place to be for **free** downloadable software to help you study for the SAT I

- Peterson's Guides is a major publisher of college handbooks, software, and related materials. Peterson's Education Center currently offers information about undergraduate education, graduate school, and summer programs, with more promised to follow soon.

- The Rezun Home College Tour at present offers only a sample of what might be the future of college admissions on the 'Net: college search, information, and application - all from the privacy of your own computer! At present only a small number of colleges are participating, but more are promised soon.

High School Web Sites

A growing number of high schools are adding their Web sites to the Internet, including helpful information on choosing a college, exploring majors and careers, and investigating financial aid opportunities. Use the search feature on your browser to locate high schools on the Net, and go to their counseling pages. The example on page 97 is what you're likely to find.

To Sum Things Up

Now you have a systematic way of identifying, organizing, and recording college information and resources on the Internet. If you spend as little as two hours on the Web expeditions outlined in this chapter, you'll probably have gathered more useful information than the average college-bound student collects in two months.

Now you're ready to move on to the next chapter and get some guidelines on using the Internet to find out about paying for college.

Financial Aid Facts and Sources on the Net

Financial Aid Quiz

	True	False
Millions of financial aid dollars go unused every year	❏	❏
Only super high-achieving students get scholarships	❏	❏
Only very low-income students qualify for financial aid	❏	❏
Only rich students can afford high-cost colleges	❏	❏

If you answered "false" to all four questions, you already know the basic realities of financial aid, but read on to find out more.

Just the Facts

Fact #1   **There Are Few, if Any, Untapped Financial Aid Bonanzas**

Nearly all financial aid money—about $47 billion in 1994-95—comes from three sources in the following amounts, with a very small percentage from a fourth source:

- 75 percent from the federal government
- 6 percent from state governments
- 18 percent from colleges and universities
- 1 percent from private sources

Fact # 2   **More than Half of All Financial Aid Comes in the Form of Loans**

Here's a breakdown of how aid is distributed:

- 43 percent is in grants and scholarships that don't have to be repaid
- 1 percent comes in the form of work-study programs that are campus based but funded by the federal government. States and institutions also offer some work-study funding
- 56 percent is in student loans

Office of Postsecondary Education

Our mission is to assist students to set and meet challenging postsecondary educational goals, and to promote excellence in postsecondary education...

FAST TRACK | **INFO FOR STUDENTS** | **INFO FOR SCHOOLS** | **EXPLORING THE WEB**

Fast Track

provides brief summaries of the OPE organization and Web pages
- Highlights of the OPE Web Site
- Official Announcements and News Releases
- Overview of Major OPE Organizations
- Directory of OPE Headquarters and Regional Offices

Information for Students

features guides on financial aid programs that can enable students to attend postsecondary educational institutions.
- The Student Guide to Federal Financial Aid Programs
- Funding Your Education
- The Direct Loan Program
- Instructions for Completing the 1996-97 Free Application for Federal Student Aid (FAFSA)
- FAFSA Express - Free Application for Federal Student Aid (downloadable software)
- State Guaranty Agencies
- State Higher Education Agencies
- Title IV School Code Search Page 1996-97

Information for Schools

describes OPE-sponsored programs and grant opportunities established to ensure excellence and equity in postsecondary education.
- Policy, Planning and Innovation
- Fund for the Improvement of Postsecondary Education
- Student Financial Assistance Programs
- Higher Education Programs
- Historically Black Colleges and Universities

Exploring the Web

consists of links to other interesting web sites on postsecondary education. *(Note: The inclusion of these sites does not necessarily mean that they are endorsed by O.P.E.)*
- ERIC Clearinghouse for Community Colleges
- Business, Trade, and Technical Schools

Fact # 3   **Most Financial Aid from the Three Primary Sources Is Need Based**

The amount of aid offered is based on evaluation of family income and assets, plus other related factors, such as family size.

Scholarships awarded strictly on the basis of high academic, athletic, or artistic ability, or minority status, are a tiny slice of the financial aid pie and usually come directly from the colleges' own funds.

Fact # 4   **Financial Aid Is Not Just For Low-Income Students**

- nearly half of all students receive some form of financial aid
- last year the average family income of students receiving financial aid was $40,000

Some families with annual incomes of over $60,000 qualified for aid, as you can see from the chart on the following page.

Fact # 5   **Every Student Should Complete the FAFSA (Free Application for Federal Student Aid)**

Why? Submitting a FAFSA is the only way to find out if you're eligible for federal financial aid.

Dependent Students at Public Colleges

Parents' Total Income	% Receiving Aid	Average Award
Less than $20,000	70.7	$3,780
$20–40,000	47.6	$3,412
$40–59,999	25.9	$3,159
$60–79,999	23.0	$3,021
$80–99,999	21.3	$3,010
$100,000 and over	14.7	$3,102

Dependent Students at Private Colleges

Parents' Total Income	% Receiving Aid	Average Award
Less than $20,000	90.9	$8,115
$20–40,000	85.2	$9,220
$40–59,999	71.7	$8,905
$60–79,999	49.0	$6,937
$80–99,999	56.0	$6,681
$100,000 and over	32.1	$5,122

Source: NAICU analysis of data for academic year 1992-93 from U.S. Department of Education

When? Immediately after January 1 of your senior year of high school (and every January while you're in college).

How long does it take to get an answer? In six to eight weeks you'll receive a SAR (Student Aid Report) that tells you the amount of federal aid, if any, that you're eligible for.

What's the point of submitting a FAFSA if your parents' income is high? If something happens in the coming year to lower your family's expected income, with a FAFSA on file, a college can quickly determine if you're now eligible for aid.

Free Application for Federal Student Aid
1996-97 School Year

WARNING: If you purposely give false or misleading information on this form, you may be fined $10,000, sent to prison, or both.

"You" and "your" on this form always mean the student who wants aid.

Form Approved
OMB No. 1845-0110
App. Exp. 6/30/97

U.S. Department of Education
Student Financial
Assistance Program

| Print in capital letters with a dark ink. | B E R 2 4 | Fill in ovals completely. | Right ● | Wrong ⊗ ✓ |

Section A: You (the student)

1–3. Your name

1. Last name
2. First name
3. M.I.

Your title (optional)   Mr. ○ 1   Miss, Mrs., or Ms. ○ 2

4–7. Your permanent mailing address
(All mail will be sent to this address. See Instructions, page 2 for state/country abbreviations.)

4. Number and street (Include apt. no.)

5. City
6. State
7. ZIP code

8. Your social security number (SSN) *(Don't leave blank. See Instructions, page 2.)*

9. Your date of birth
Month   Day   Year

10. Your permanent home telephone number
Area code

11. Your state of legal residence
State

12. Date you became a legal resident of the state in question 11
(See Instructions, page 2.)
Month   Day   Year

13–14. Your driver's license number *(Include the state abbreviation. If you don't have a license, write in "None.")*
State   License number

15–16. Are you a U.S. citizen?
(See Instructions, pages 2–3.)
Yes, I am a U.S. citizen.   ○ 1
No, but I am an eligible noncitizen.   ○ 2
A
No, neither of the above.   ○ 3

17. As of today, are you married? *(Fill in only one oval.)*
I am not married. (I am single, widowed, or divorced.)   ○ 1
I am married.   ○ 2
I am separated from my spouse.   ○ 3

18. Date you were married, separated, divorced, or widowed. If divorced, use date of divorce or separation, whichever is earlier.
(If never married, leave blank.)
Month   Year

19. Will you have your first bachelor's degree before July 1, 1996?   Yes ○ 1   No ○ 2

Section B: Education Background

20–21. Date that you (the student) received, or will receive, your high school diploma, either—
Month   Year
• by graduating from high school
OR
Month   Year
• by earning a GED
(Enter one date. Leave blank if the question does not apply to you.)

22–23. Highest educational level or grade level your father and your mother completed. *(Fill in one oval for each parent. See Instructions, page 3.)*

	22. Father	23. Mother
elementary school (K–8)	○ 1	○ 1
high school (9–12)	○ 2	○ 2
college or beyond	○ 3	○ 3
unknown	○ 4	○ 4

If you (and your family) have unusual circumstances, complete this form and then check with your financial aid administrator. Examples:
• tuition expenses at an elementary or secondary school,
• unusual medical or dental expenses not covered by insurance,
• a family member who recently became unemployed, or
• other unusual circumstances such as changes in income or assets that might affect your eligibility for student financial aid.

| Fact # 6 | **Never Rule Out a College Because of Cost** |

If your family's annual income exceeds $60,000, the odds are you're not going to get much in the way of federal assistance. But don't let that stop you from applying to a college because it costs more than your family can afford. Many colleges with high tuition, room, and board costs have substantial endowment funds that enable them to meet the financial aid needs of students who don't qualify for federal funds. Those colleges use a need analysis formula that takes into account factors such as home equity and unusually high medical or dental expenses.

The form that many private colleges require or recommend for determining eligibility for nonfederal financial aid is the CSS/Financial Aid PROFILE. Approximately 450 colleges and universities, and a similar number of private scholarship programs, ask applicants to complete the PROFILE, which has priority filing dates that differ from the FAFSA application date. Ask your high school counselor for a PROFILE registration guide or register online by going to:

http://www.collegeboard.org/profile.html

For more information on federal financial aid, tips for completing a FAFSA, and/or to download and submit a FAFSA, see FAFSA Express below and go to:

http://www.ed.gov/prog_info/SFA/FAFSA/

Some Good Web Sites for Basic Financial Aid (Also see Appendix D)

The Ambitious Student's Guide to Financial Aid by Robert and Anna Lieder
http://www.signet.com/collegemoney/

FAFSA Express

What is FAFSA Express?

It's free. It's fast. It's easy.

FAFSA Express makes the paperless financial aid application a reality. A PC equipped with the Windows® operating system and a modem can transmit an electronic Free Application for Federal Student Aid (FAFSA) to the Department of Education. *FAFSA Express* users enjoy the benefits of Electronic Data Exchange, such as eliminating delays from mailing and ensuring a faster receipt of an official Expected Family Contribution from the Department. The software also speeds up the application process by automatically checking electronic FAFSA data, resulting in fewer rejected applications.

Use it at home or at school.

Because *FAFSA Express* is designed for applicants, it has an easy-to-use Windows® interface and extensive on-line instructions for completing the application. Help with all of the application's questions is available with a single click of your mouse.

1996–97 FAFSA Express Downloading Instructions

Current version is 2.1

Questions about downloading the FAFSA Express from the WWW should be addressed to *FAFSA_ADMIN@ed.gov*. The Department has also established a customer service line for *FAFSA Express* users. If you need assistance with hardware, software, or transmission, or if you want to check the status of your application after you complete and submit your electronic FAFSA contact the *FAFSA Express* Customer Service Line at 1-(800)-801-0576.

*** last update May 01, 1996 (krc/eal) ***

_###_

Return to OPE Home Page

College Board Online
http://www.collegeboard.org

CollegeView
http://www.collegeview.com

Financial Aid Information Page by Mark Kantrowitz
(now sponsored by NASFAA)
http://www.finaid.org/

The Student Guide to Financial Aid 1995-1996 provided
by the U.S. Department of Education
http://inet.ed.gov/prog_info/SFA/StudentGuide

UCLA Financial Aid Page
http://www.gse.ucla.edu/mm/cc/links/aid.html

USBank
http://usbanksl.com/aid/faq2.html

Also check out online newspapers and magazines, such as
Money Magazine, *U.S. News*, and *USA Today*. Search the publication's archives using key words—college financial aid,
scholarships, etc.—to find articles and columns that may
include useful advice.

Keep in mind that the SEARCH option on your Web browser
is a very helpful tool for locating information using key words.

The Best Surprise Is No Surprise

While you can't file for federal financial aid until January 1 of
the year in which you'll be using it, there's no need to wait
until then to get a rough idea of what, if any, federal funds
you'll be eligible for. It only makes sense that the more time
you have to plan and save, the better financial shape you'll be

The Student Guide

Financial Aid from the U.S. Department of Education (ED)

The Student Guide supplements a wide range of publications which are available upon request from the ED Office of Postsecondary Education (OPE).

If you should have any questions about the Guide, or wish to obtain additional information on student financial assistance, you may contact your high school guidance counselor, the financial aid officer at the postsecondary education institution you plan to attend, or by calling ED's toll free student information hotline at 1-800-4-FED-AID.

The Student Guide 1996-97 This document provides information about student financial assistance for the 1996-97 award year. This award year begins on July 1, 1996 and ends on June 30, 1997. Read this document for more information about aid you might receive for the 1996-97 school year. Check with your school to find out which award year summer terms belong to.

The Student Guide 1995-96 This document provides information about student financial assistance for the 1995-96 award year. This award year began on July 1, 1995 and ends on June 30, 1996. Read this document for more information about aid you might receive for the 1995-96 school year. Check with your school to find out which award year summer terms belong to.

*** last updated 2/29/96 (earlier)

_***_

in when it's time to pay the first tuition bill. A good way to begin your financial planning is to complete an Expected Family Contribution (EFC) worksheet. Web sites where you can download an EFC form or complete one online are listed below.

Expected Family Contribution Form

Your Expected Family Contribution (EFC) is the total amount you and your family are expected to pay toward college costs from income and assets. The amount is derived from a need analysis of the family's overall financial circumstances.

Estimate your Expected Family Contribution instantaneously using this free service.

| home | search | store | library | communication | help |

Web Sites with Expected Family Contribution Worksheets

> http://www.collegeboard.org/css/html/indx001.html
> http://www.finaid.org/
> http://www.salliemae.com/calculators/efc/

The EFC worksheet for federal financial aid applies the methodology used in the FAFSA to determine what a family is able, and therefore required, to contribute to the cost of their child's college education. The computations are based on the figures from your family's most recent federal tax return, and your Expected Family Contribution remains constant regardless of the cost of the college you attend.

In other words, if your EFC is $4,000 and you apply to a college with annual costs of $10,000, your federal financial

110

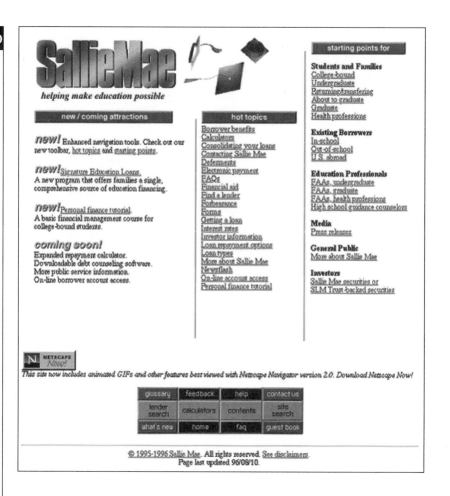

aid eligibility will be $6,000. If you apply to a college that costs $17,000 per year, your federal eligibility will be $13,000. Eligibility, however, is not a guarantee that you'll receive that amount. It's up to the college to determine whether they can provide all, part, or none of the financial aid for which you're eligible.

How the Expected Family Contribution Formula Works

College A

$10,000 = Annual Cost
 of Attendance

− $4,000 = Family Contribution

$6,000 = Financial Need

College B

$17,000 = Annual Cost
 of Attendance

− $4,000 = Family Contribution

$13,000 = Financial Need

Why Cost Should Not Be Your Primary Consideration

Typical Financial Aid Package

$4,000 bank loan

$1,500 work study

$500 grant

Typical Financial Aid Package

$4,000 bank loan

$3,000 work study

$6,000 grant

Out-of-Pocket Cost

$4,000

Out-of-Pocket Cost

$4,000

A Few Facts About the Financial Aid Package

Your financial aid package at an expensive college may make that college as affordable as your state university or a less expensive private college, so don't rule out a college that interests you because of its cost. Be sure to look carefully at the financial aid information at the Web site of any college you're considering to find out what forms are required and when the deadlines are.

Once your financial aid application forms have been processed and you've been accepted for admission, the college will send you a letter outlining the amount and type of financial aid they are prepared to offer you to meet your financial need. Financial need is defined as the cost of attendance (tuition, room and board, books, etc.) minus the dollar amount your family is able to contribute, as determined by the required need analysis forms you submitted.

Your financial aid package is likely to be a combination of:

- grant money (state, federal, and, perhaps, institutional funds that do not have to be repaid)
- self-help dollars (an on-campus job to help you pay your share of the cost)
- subsidized loan (money that will have to be repaid, with interest, when you complete or leave college)

While colleges strive to meet your full financial need, some can't, and you may need to find additional sources of funding to finance your education. There are a growing number of Web sites that offer valuable information about where and how to look for private financial aid dollars.

The Money Hunt

Scholarships

You can gather a lot of free information. Start with your own school or public library, which may have a scholarship search software program that you can use at no cost. Also do a thorough search on the Web, which gives you access to a number of online data bases with scholarship information.

Caution

Be wary of companies that claim there are millions of dollars in scholarship money going unused, charge a fee for doing a college scholarship search, and promise you the names and addresses of dozens of sources. Often what you get is nothing more than what's available free on the Web or at your library. Mark Kantrowitz, a financial aid adviser at Carnegie Mellon University, advises that you avoid companies that:

- make statements or promises of guaranteed winnings
- suggest or claim that everyone is eligible
- pressure you to respond quickly to their offer
- request unusual personal/financial information
- require a high application fee
- have typing and spelling errors in their brochure or application

See Appendix D for reliable college scholarship information.

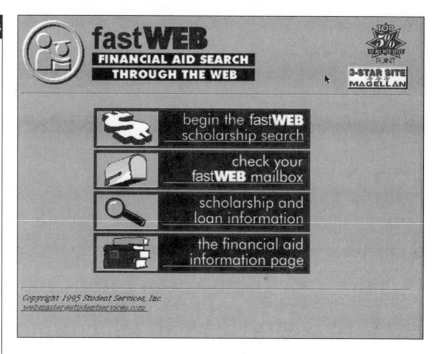

Loans

It's likely that you, like many other students, are going to have to borrow to pay for some portion of your college expenses. Nearly half of recent college graduates left their alma mater with an average bank loan of $10,000 to repay out of future earnings. The key is learning how to manage your debt and, in some cases, consolidate your loans to simplify your repayment.

You can find a number of Web sites that provide information on student loans. Not surprisingly, some of the better ones have been developed by commercial banks, which have a vested interest in you as a potential client for their

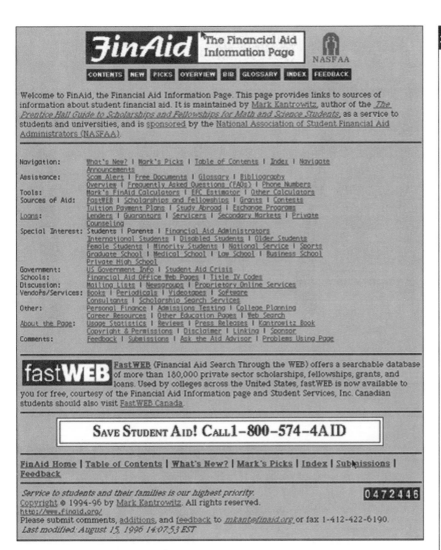

student loan services. Some sites offer help in calculating the monthly cost (principal, interest, and fees) of a hypothetical loan amount. Other sites provide a forum to discuss loans with other students and their families.

financial.aid services

College Board online

Financial Aid Information and Services for Students and Parents

Information for all students and parents:

- Understanding college costs and financial aid
- Compute your expected family contribution online. It's free!
- CSS College Savings Adviser. *Complete the brief questionnaire online and see how your savings can grow between now and the time your child enters college. It's free!*
- CSS/College Money PLANNER: *It takes the mystery out of meeting college costs!*
  - Learn about the CSS/College Money PLANNER. You tell us about your finances and we tell you how much you might receive in financial aid, how much you may be expected to contribute, and strategies for meeting your share of college costs through savings, borrowing, and cash.
  - Complete CSS/College Money PLANNER questionnaire and submit it online!
- Borrowing for education
- Bibliography on paying for college
- Glossary of financial and financial aid terms

Information for high school seniors, enrolled college students, and their parents:

- Register for the CSS/Financial Aid PROFILE online if you are applying for financial aid from any of more than 800 colleges and scholarship programs for the 1996-97 award year.

Go to College Board Financial Aid Services Directory

---

home   search   store   library   communication   help

This entire site protected by copyright. All rights reserved. By accessing and using this site, you agree to be subject to the "Terms and Conditions Governing Use and Access to College Board Online."

Other Sources of Financial Aid Information

State Agencies

Every state has a higher education agency that regulates and awards financial aid to its residents. Some have a Web page on the Internet. Be sure to contact your state agency, by con-

Borrowing for Education

COLLEGECREDIT

- Financial Planning and Borrowing Tips and Tools for Parents
- Financial Planning and Borrowing Tips and Tools for Students
- Student and Parent Loans Available from the CollegeCredit Program

Financial Planning and Borrowing Tips and Tools for Parents

- **General Planning Information**
  - o Financial Planning Tips
  - o Debt Planning Worksheet for Parents
  - o Parent Loan Adviser. Calculate online how much you can afford to borrow, based on your income and current debt repayments!
  - o Parent Loan Repayment Calculator. Calculate online what your monthly loan repayment would be if you borrow from the PLUS or other parent loan programs. It's free.
  - o Parents' Net Worth Worksheet
- **Explore the Parent Loans for Undergraduate Students (PLUS) Program**
  - o A Parent's Guide to PLUS Loans and Credit Reports
  - o Parent's Guide to the CollegeCredit PLUS Loan
  - o Sample Repayment Schedule under Federal PLUS Program (Parent Loans)

Financial Planning Tips and Tools for Students

- **What you should know about student loans**
  - o Guide to Responsible Borrowing
  - o Financial "Rules of Thumb" for Students: Debt and Budgeting Guidelines
  - o Student Loan Adviser. Calculate whether your student loan repayment is likely to be manageable using the College Board's online Student Loan Adviser. It's free!
  - o How to Choose a Student Loan Lender
  - o Cut your costs for borrowing Subsidized Federal Stafford Loans
  - o Monthly Repayments under Federal Stafford Loan Program (Student Loans)
  - o Cost Comparison: Subsidized and Unsubsidized Federal Stafford Loans
  - o Consolidating Your Education Loans
  - o Who Owns Your Student Loan?
  - o When Your Student Loan is Sold
- **Financial Tips for Students**
  - o Making the Most of Your Money: Tips for Students
  - o Student Guide to Record Keeping
  - o Balancing your Checkbook
  - o Credit Card Smarts
  - o Credit Card and Calling Card Safety
  - o Estimated Starting Incomes for College Grads

Go to Financial Aid Services for Students and Parents Directory
Go to Financial Aid Services for Counselors Directory
Go to College Board Financial Aid Services Directory

home   search   store   library   communication   help

Welcome To Citibank Student Loans

Where getting money for college can be easier than you think...

Financing a college education shouldn't be a complicated process and here at Citibank we've tried to simplify the process to help students and parents navigate the maze of financial aid.

If you're looking for an affordable way to pay for college, look no further than Citibank. We have over 30 years of experience helping students finance college.

Whether you are interested in loans for undergraduate or graduate school, chances are Citibank has a federally guaranteed student loan to fit your needs. Options are provided below to help you find the information you need. The information provided at this web site is meant as an introduction and overview to loan options. For complete information, please fill out our Online Request Form; call Citibank at 1-800-692-8200, and ask for Operator 144; or stop by your local branch and pick up a loan application kit.

Citibank Stafford and Citi Assist Loans are available to schools participating in the Federal Family Education Loan (FFEL) program. Citi Assist Loans for graduate students are available to students attending schools participating in the Federal Direct Student Loan (FDSL) programs.

Options for College Undergraduates and Their Parents

Citibank offers several federal loan options for both undergraduate students and their parents. These options are outlined here.

Options for Graduate Students

In addition to federal loans, Citibank has created several special loan options just for students entering graduate school. There is a Citibank graduate loan that's right for you.

ventional mail or on the Web, to request information about
all financial aid programs available in your state. The Net
address to find your state's Higher Education Agency online
is as follows:

http://www.ed.gov/offices/OPE/agencies.html

Financial Aid Officers

The best source of information on financial aid at a specific
college is that college's Web site. Look there to find answers
to the following questions:

- What percentage of freshmen received some type of
  loan, grant, or work aid?
- What was the average dollar amount of each?
- Is the institution's financial aid policy for first-year students different from the policy for upperclassmen? If
  so, in what way does it differ?
- Could I expect a comparable financial aid package,
  assuming my financial need remains comparable, for
  each year that I'm enrolled and in good standing?
- What is the average loan burden of graduating
  students?
- What percentage of students have their full need met?
  If financial need is only partially covered, does the
  college provide help in identifying other funding
  sources to meet remaining costs?
- What is the college's policy about offering admission
  if financial aid is not available?

- Do Early Decision applicants have a better chance of getting financial aid?

If you can't locate all the information you're looking for, you may want to get in touch with the director of financial aid (DFA) at that college. Using e-mail on the Internet, you have a quick, direct way to contact the person (see the following sample message).

TO: financial aid office@college.edu
FROM: your name@xxx.com
Subject: Can You Help Me?

Message:

Hi, I'm seriously considering applying to your college this fall. Could you and/or a member of your staff please take a few minutes to answer the following questions:

(List briefly the questions you haven't been able to answer on your own.)

Thank you for taking the time to respond.

your name
high school name
home phone number
(if you'd like to be contacted by phone)

Financial Aid Newsgroups

Try using your browser to locate newsgroups on financial aid. Most of the commercial ISPs have newsgroups on this subject where students and parents can share their concerns about paying for college, discuss strategies for doing so, and exchange helpful information.

Chapter 7

Putting Your College Search in Perspective

At this point, you probably have collected a lot of information from college home pages and people on the Net. As you review it, some of it may seem too subjective or "hard sell" to be useful. Other parts may seem confusing or contradictory. Now it's time to sort through the information, to separate the fluff from the facts, and to put your college search in perspective.

Subjective vs. Objective Information

It's safe to say that up to 70 percent of the information on the Internet is subjective—that is, based more on personal opinion than on verifiable facts and figures. Both subjective and objective information need to be evaluated carefully, keeping the following guidelines in mind:

Base your conclusions on a range of opinions rather than those of one person or one group. College faculty, administrators, and matriculated students often have significantly different points of view about what is "good" or "bad" in teaching practices, campus life, colleagues/fellow students, academic support systems, etc. Put your critical thinking skills to work in comparing, contrasting, and evaluating the wide range of information you've gathered.

Look for patterns rather than focusing on isolated pieces of information/opinion. For example, if the majority of students you've contacted at a particular college report that they love their institution, and a number of alumni echo that feeling, you can be fairly confident that the college is consistent in servicing its students' needs. On the other hand, if you get sharply differing, contradictory opinions, it would be a good idea to investigate further and weigh those opinions in light of your own likes, dislikes, and needs.

Use a "red flag" and "green light" technique to separate a college's negatives from its positives. By marking the plus and minus factors on your WWW worksheets with red and green highlighter, you can quickly create visual guidelines for evaluating the schools you're considering.

Be wary of hidden agendas. Information about a course from a student who flunked it may not be reliable. It's not always easy, or worth the effort, to pinpoint an individual's bias, so try getting several people's responses to the same subject, and some basic facts may emerge.

Take note of when information at a particular Web site was last updated. Not all sites are updated regularly, and you want to make decisions based on the most current data available. It's a good idea to go back to a site periodically (use your bookmarks to do that quickly and easily) to see "what's new."

Consult with your counselor and other professionals. Take your Web worksheets to your school counselor to discuss your progress, observations, and concerns. The admission staff at many colleges are reachable by e-mail and can give you a lot of useful information and advice. Remember that you have a wide network of people on the Web who are ready and willing to help you.

Be realistic in your expectations. Not everyone will have the time or inclination to respond promptly (or at all) to your e-mail. A particular professor may be working around the clock to meet a publishing deadline and at the same time to keep up with teaching, testing, and grading responsibilities. Remember that the number of e-mail exchanges on the Internet is growing geometrically.

College admission offices reported that between 1994 and 1995 there was an increase of 350 percent in e-mail messages received from students. To keep up with that volume, some admission offices now batch all e-mail received and assign a different staff member each day to respond to all inquiries. Don't be offended if your message is answered by someone other than the person you addressed it to. It's the information that counts.

Visit the colleges that you're most interested in whenever possible. You can use e-mail to prearrange a meeting with a group of students or faculty. A virtual tour on the Net is good, but nothing takes the place of a walk around the campus, a firsthand look at the dorms, auditing a class session, and eating in the student cafeteria. When you go, be sure to take along your WWW worksheet to remind you about any unanswered questions and to compare your red flag/green light evaluations against your experiences on campus.

Compare your needs and wants with the results of your Net search. A truly useful college search involves not only objective evaluations of prospective institutions, but a careful assessment of your personal interests, strengths, weaknesses, quirks, and unique needs. Ask yourself the following questions, and compare your answers with the information you've gathered:

What are my career goals and/or intended major? (Did my Web search give me adequate information on the strengths and limitations of various academic programs?)

Where do I see myself in five years? (Did I get the information I need about the career planning and placement services at each college? Degrees offered? Requirements for graduation?)

What are my academic strengths and limitations?
(How complete is my research on the academic climate on campus? Do I know as much as I need to about the course work? What did students have to say about their courses and instructors? Are there tutorial services available on campus?)

What activities are most important to me outside the daily routine of school? (Did I find out enough about what student groups and clubs are available at each college? Do I have an accurate sense of what extracurricular resources are close enough to each campus to meet my needs?)

What kind of academic setting is best for me? (Did I get the information I need about class size? Types of assignments in freshman-level courses? Types of exams given in freshman-level courses?)

What are my parents' expectations? (Did I get the information I need about financial aid? How convenient/costly is it to get to and from college? What about campus security? Health services?)

Narrowing and Sorting Your Choices

Your logical next step is to sort your top 8 to 12 colleges into one of three categories:

Stretch schools

These are institutions where your qualifications might not meet all their admission standards. You might not have taken enough Advanced Placement/honors courses, or your grade-point average might be a few points shy of their average, or your teacher recommendations might be lukewarm, or your SAT/ACT scores might be slightly below the range of scores for their typical freshman class. Whatever the case, you know the odds are long, but it's worth a shot. No more than a third of your prospective colleges should fall into this category.

Probable schools

These are institutions where you meet the admission criteria but, depending on the competition when you apply, you can't be absolutely certain you will be admitted (for instance, if you're applying to the most popular campus of your state university or applying to a particularly strong state university as a nonresident of that state). In other words, you're about 90 percent sure that you'll be accepted if you apply. A third to a half of your prospective colleges should fall into this category.

Safety schools

These are institutions where you meet or surpass all the admission criteria and you're 100 percent certain you'll gain admission. You may decide to limit this category to one or two colleges, but be sure they're places that you're convinced you will like, where you will be able to achieve your academic goals.

Unsure if you've put a prospective college in the correct category? Do a little further investigation on the Internet. Send an e-mail to a group of freshmen at that college asking them to share their high school record (SAT/ACT scores, class rank, grade-point average) and the names of other colleges that accepted them. You can also check to find out if the admission office will give you the e-mail addresses of enrolled students from your high school.

The Good News

Keep in mind the following reassuring statistics:

- nearly 80 percent of applicants are admitted to their first-choice college
- about 95 percent of students are accepted at one of their top two choices
- more than 50 percent of all four-year colleges accept 70 percent or more of their freshman applicants

Make no mistake—it's a buyer's market.

Applying for Admission Online

More than 300 colleges now have their undergraduate and/or graduate admission applications online. Some colleges let you download the application and mail it to the admission office. Other colleges let you complete and submit the applications online. In fact, some colleges waive the application fee if you apply on the Net. Still other colleges have agreements with organizations such as the College Board or CollegeView to provide electronic applications to students and transmit them electronically to the college when completed. Regardless of how you decide to submit your application, be sure to have your counselor review a printout of the completed application before you submit it online or through the mail.

Testing Reality

A *New York Times* article published in September of 1995 rocked the college admission community and surprised a lot of college-bound students. It revealed the names of colleges, including some very prestigious ones, that fudged the SAT score information they reported to prospective students to make their college appear more selective than it actually was. Many students and parents discovered through reading that article what experienced counselors have known for years—that all information about a college should be scrutinized carefully and, wherever possible, verified by an impartial source.

As the quantity of official and unofficial information about colleges keeps growing on the Internet, it becomes increasingly important to hone your critical and analytical skills. It's equally important to keep your high school counselor in the loop. The Internet can support and expand, but not supplant, the benefits of working with an experienced counselor through the college selection process.

Chapter 8

Choosing a Major and Building a Career Network on the Net

Some people may think this should have been the first chapter in the book. They are the same people who have asked you since age five, "What do you want to be when you grow up?" They can't imagine students deciding on a college without first knowing what they want to major in or do after graduation. But you may not have a clue—and that's okay. You're actually in the majority. More than half of all freshmen start college without a declared major, and the average college student changes majors twice before graduating.

So don't worry if you haven't decided yet on a major or a career. You have a year or two before your college will require you to declare your major. On the other hand, it's never too early to begin exploring possible academic and career directions, so take advantage of what the Net has to offer.

Benefit by Browsing the Net

On the Net you can:

- take and score a career interest inventory
- find out what jobs are in demand through the U.S. Labor Department
- locate and talk to employers and college students in your field of interest
- get career advice from professionals in the workplace and on college campuses
- apply for internships (paid and volunteer) within organizations located near the college of your choice

Step 1   **Start with Yourself**

If you've not taken a career or personal interest test within the past two years, it's time to do it now, either at school or on the Web. The goal is to match your abilities and interests with a range of majors and careers. Here are a few sites on the Net where you can take a career interest inventory, explore career possibilities, and get career advice. For a more complete list, see Appendix B.

CareerMosaic: The most complete single location for information about jobs, internships, and career assessment. Go directly to their College Connection page. There are hypertext links to a number of college career centers, so be sure to browse those as well.

http://www.careermosaic.com

The Career Planning Process by Pam Allen and Ellen Nagy: Another site that offers an online career-interest assessment.

http://www.cba.bgsu.edu/class/webclass/nagye/career/process.html

Career Services, University of Waterloo: Online career-interest survey.

http://www.adm.uwaterloo.ca:80/infocecs/CRC/
manual-home.html

CareerWeb: Giant data base of employers that includes a job-related self-assessment.

http://www.cweb.com

College Board Online: Go to ExPAN and browse the careers and related majors data bases as well as take the interest inventory.

http://www.collegeboard.org/expan/html/

FutureScan: Helps students take a close look at different occupations by reading the profiles of people currently working in the field and by sending e-mail questions to working professionals.

http://www.futurescan.com

The Keirsey Temperament Sorter by David Keirsey is a personality test that scores results according to the Meyers-Briggs system.

http://sunsite.unc.edu/jembin/mb.pl

Planning a Career: Assess your skills and interests, and develop a career plan online.

http://www.tgslc.org/adventur/planning.htm

If you can spare the time, take two or three different inventories. You may get a broader perspective by doing that. It's also a good idea to bounce your results off your school counselor, favorite teacher, best friend, and parents to get their feedback. While you might not agree with what they have to say, it's important to get other people's opinions of your strengths and limitations.

Step 2   ## Ask and Listen

Who knows more about the day-to-day demands, frustrations, and fun of studying biology than a senior-year biology major? Who knows more about what skills and interests it takes to succeed in accounting than a Certified Public Accountant? To get the best information, go to people who have firsthand experience.

The Internet enables you to reach out to a network of experts. Here's how:

E-mail

When exploring a college's Web site, hunt for students who share your interest in a specific subject, major, or career area. If the college doesn't list students by major, go to the academic department's home page to see if names and e-mail addresses are listed. If not there, try the home page of a special-interest group or club related to the subject you're considering.

It's good to have several names and addresses, but all you

University of Waterloo

Career Development Manual: Electronic Edition

University of Waterloo

© *Career Development Manual* may be duplicated, with credit, for educational or non-profit uses only. All other uses are prohibited without express written permission.

We hope that you find our pages to be useful, however, if you are not affiliated with the University of Waterloo (student, alumni, staff, faculty) we cannot offer you additional service by way of online career planning assistance. Emailed queries will not be answered unless a UW affiliation is made clear.

STEPS TO THE RIGHT JOB

Start at the bottom and work up

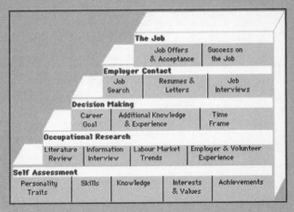

A non-graphical representation is also available if the above imagemap does not appear using your browser.

Career Development Manual Credits

We have been rated in the top 5% of internet sites by Point Survey

Occupational Outlook Handbook

1996-97 Occupational Outlook Handbook

Perform a Keyword Search on the *Handbook*

50 Years in Print

Message from the Secretary of Labor

Foreword by the Commissioner of Labor Statistics

Guide to the *Handbook*

Acknowledgements

Contents

- The Outlook for Specific Occupations
- Contacts for Data Users
- Special Features
  - Tomorrow's Jobs
  - Sources of Career Information
  - Finding a Job and Evaluating a Job Offer
  - Occupational Information Included in the *Handbook*
  - Data for Occupations Not Studied in Detail
  - Assumptions and Methods Used in Preparing Employment Projections
  - Reprints

Related Publications

- *Occupational Projections and Training Data*
- *Occupational Outlook Quarterly*
- *Employment Outlook: 1994-2005*

Employment Projections Home Page

Publications Home Page

BLS Home Page

Howard N Fullerton, Jr
Bureau of Labor Statistics
Pilot.Mobis.gov
Last modified: July 15, 1996
URL: http://stats.bls.gov/occhome.htm

need is one to get the ball rolling. From there you can ask that one person to forward your e-mail to other students. Here are a few questions you may want to ask:

- How and why did you select your major? Are you happy with your decision?
- What courses have you taken?
- What do you plan to do after graduation?
- What have classmates in your major done after graduation? Kinds of jobs? Type of graduate school?
- What's the job outlook for graduates with your degree?
- What advice would you give a high school student interested in your major?

Engineering Undergraduate Council

Welcome to the Penn State Engineering Undergraduate Council (EUC) World Wide Web page. EUC is the students' most active voice in the College of Engineering. With our seats on Engineering Roundtable, Faculty Council, Academic Assembly, University Faculty Senate, and Engineering Undergraduate Student Advisory Committee, we are an integral part of this insitution.

Officers:
- President: Marie Yingling
- Vice President: Jim Clark
- Secretary: John Chinnici
- Treasurer: Mike Goodman
- Engineering Roundtable Chairs:
  - Rachel Kusza
  - Susan Hwang
- University Faculty Senator: John Groenveld
- Engineering Faculty Council:
  - Kevin Monroe
  - Josh Keir
- Hosting Chair: Melissa Morehouse
- Past President: Marianne Ocampo

Calendar
T-Shirt Design Competition

John D. Groenveld <groenvel@cse.psu.edu>
Last update: Wed May 29 17:14:10 EDT 1996

Don't hesitate to contact professors by e-mail to ask similar questions. Faculty are in a position to give you insight into career opportunities as well as to tell you about the academic demands. They can also tell you what specialties are "hot" in their field and what kinds of courses and other preparation are required to land a good job or for acceptance in a top graduate program.

E-mail is also a great way of contacting working professionals and employers to learn more about the jobs and profession. You can ask employees questions such as:

- Why did you choose your line of work?
- Where did you go to college? What was your degree?
- What do you enjoy the most and least about your work?
- What skills are essential in your work?
- What major is the best preparation for the work you do?
- What special course work is recommended?

You can ask employers questions such as:

- What skills, course work, and degrees do you look for?
- Approximately how many entry-level jobs do you fill each year?
- Is your organization expanding?
- What's the outlook for advancement in your field?

The best place to find names and e-mail addresses of employees and employers is where they meet online, such as the employment section of online newspapers, Web sites where job seekers post their resumes, and newsgroups. You can also search the membership of your Net provider using occupational key words (accountant, physician) to identify fellow members willing to share their thoughts and recommendations.

Newsgroups

Another way to contact working professionals online is through newsgroups. Newsgroups bring hundreds, sometimes thousands, of people together to discuss topics of mutual interest. Anyone on the Net interested in discussing that topic can post a question or comment on the newsgroup's bulletin board for others to read and respond to. Most professional associations (American Dental Association, American Bar Association, National Education Association) have newsgroups and bulletin boards on their Web sites.

Step 3   Networking on the Net

If you want to get off to a quick start and move ahead in a career, it helps to have a network of people ready to steer you in the right direction, give you the benefit of their experience, and put you in touch with some of the "movers and shakers" in your field. Let's face it. No one wants to graduate from college with $25,000–$75,000 in student loans and flip hamburgers for a living because they can't find a job or a graduate program in their field. The marketplace is changing every year. The jobs in demand today might not be around tomorrow.

USENET SEARCH

Get Your Fresh, Hot Jobs!

We are averaging over 57,000 postings daily from the top USENET newsgroups, and our index is rebuilt every 24 hours on a rolling basis. The postings are always current, as we expire them every seven days. With so many postings, the more specific you can be, the more relevant the response will be.

For your information, USENET is a collection of newsgroups distributed electronically around the world. Also known as USENET Newsgroups, USENET can be thought of as a world wide bulletin board system with newsgroups numbering in the thousands. CareerMosaic indexes the newsgroups that are of interest to the job seeker and recruiting department thereby saving you a great deal of time. USENET is not an organization and therefore no one person or group is in charge of it as a whole, rather, many USENET sites are at universities and a large number of sites are now commercial organizations.

To begin, use the search box below. An "ideal" search might be: "UNIX and New and York," which would find jobs mentioning UNIX and New York. You have to use "and" between each word since the search uses "or" as the default. Select a state or province from the scroll box on the right to find opportunities in the area of interest to you (your choice will be added as an "and" to your search criteria; you may select "No Location" if you wish).

Go to J.O.B.S. Also go to our CareerMosaic J.O.B.S. (Job Opportunities By Search) page. You'll find thousands of jobs from hundreds of top employers in high tech, health care, finance, retailing, and other fields. It's a CareerMosaic exclusive!

Search for: [   ] [Submit] | No Location |
| Alabama |
| Alaska |
| Alberta |

CAREERMOSAIC HOME   EMPLOYERS   J.O.B.S.   INFO

It's Never Too Early

To ensure that you won't end up unemployed or underemployed after graduation, you need to start planning at the beginning of your college career. That means developing a network of people (on- and offline) who are willing to be mentors and guides, and developing a resume (on- and offline) that demonstrates your accomplishments.

To land a job with great potential, it's not necessarily what you know, but who you know. So start building your network early, because one of your mentors today may be the person interviewing you for your dream job tomorrow.

Cyberguides to the Rescue

In college you will be assigned an academic adviser, whose responsibility is to help you select the right courses in order to graduate. That adviser will be very important, but not the only person to rely on as a guide. Start now, even before you get to college, to seek out people who understand your interests and are qualified to offer career advice when needed.

You could think of them as "Net pals," an electronic version of pen pals. All you need to do is ask the people you think will enhance your network if they would be willing to keep in touch and occasionally provide advice or answers to your career-related questions. You'll be surprised at how many senior professionals are willing to share their experience and expertise with a college student, perhaps because they remember what it was like to be in your shoes at one time.

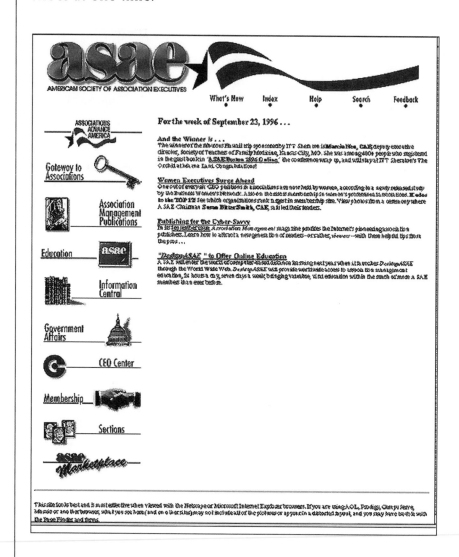

Online Resume

It's never too soon to prepare a resume, and there are many places on the Net to get free advice on building a resume as well as some sites that will critique your resume. Most college career planning and placement offices offer good advice on their Web sites, but also check out the following address:

Online Career Center (http://www.occ.com/occ)

A growing number of Net users are developing their own personal home pages and putting their resumes online. Colleges report that more and more students are including the Web address of their personal home page on their admission application. With Net technology you can even present a multimedia resume by adding video and sound. This is particularly useful if you're applying for a graphic or performing arts scholarship since it enables you to demonstrate your talents online as part of your personal home page.

Cyber-U

It wasn't much more than a decade ago that desktop computers began replacing typewriters. At that time, the idea of students sitting at personal computers in their own homes, communicating with professors via an electronic network accessed by a modem and phone line and completing college courses for credit without attending classes seemed more like science fiction than scientific fact. But distance learning, as it's called, is now a reality. Reputable and accredited

institutions, among them the University of Maryland, the University of Rochester, Pennsylvania State University, the University of Phoenix, and the University of Iowa, offer courses on the Internet that span the curriculum, from psychology to microeconomics, and grant degrees or certificates for successful completion of those courses.

You're probably looking forward to actually being in college, attending classes, having one-on-one discussions with your

HEADLINES

OCC's NEW SYSTEM TO BE RELEASED SOON!!!
Oracle Database Management System and New Features Included

OCC WELCOMES NEW MEMBER CORPORATIONS!!!!

MEMBER COMPANIES MAY ENTER 'HTML' ADS INTO THE DATABASE!
Add color, graphics, links, e-mail connectivity, and more!!

ENGINEERING OPPORTUNITIES IN SINGAPORE
Venture Manufacturing (Singapore) - Top rated by Forbes Magazine

CAREER FAIRS ON ONLINE CAREER CENTER
Thompson Virtual Job Fair and many others!!!

JOIN THE MCI INTERNET DIGERATI !!!
MCI's Internet Network Development Team, Reston, VA

DATA PROCESSING PROFESSIONALS NEEDED IN THE PACIFIC NORTHWEST!

FAQ | Home | Join | Jobs | Resumes | Recruiter's Office | Career Assistance | On Campus | Help

Online Career Center, occ@occ.com

Copyright(c) 1996 - Online Career Center LP -- All Rights Reserved

Manager of Internet Services - Renee Ahrbecker
System Administration - David Thompson

Best if viewed through
NETSCAPE *Now!*

professors, getting to know the other students, and becoming a part of the campus community. But keep in mind that distance learning can be combined with a more traditional approach.It's a good way to strengthen your academic preparation and an economical way to earn some of the credits you need for graduation. It also gives you an opportunity to take courses that may not be available at your college or any

148 nearby. With the Internet, a student on the East Coast can take a course at a college on the West Coast and still have lots of interaction with far-flung fellow students via real-time conferencing and e-mail.

In many ways, the "virtual classroom" parallels the traditional classroom. Both offer a direct dialogue between the instructor and the student, both facilitate interaction between students, have comparable reading requirements, and assess learning through term papers and/or tests. Some virtual classes are conducted live (real-time interaction between students and instructor), while some classes are conducted asynchronously (the instructor electronically posts the assignments and students pace themselves using e-mail to return completed requirements).In nearly all distance learning courses, students are required to use the full services of the Internet (bulletin boards, World Wide Web, chat rooms, newsgroups) to master the subject.

To locate colleges offering courses on the Net, use the following address and talk with your academic adviser:

Yahoo: The most widely used site for more information on distance or online learning.
http://www.yahoo.com/Education
/Alternative/Distance_Learning/

While no one knows for certain what the Internet will look like in three to five years, there are a few points on which everyone can agree:

Access to the Internet will become easier and cheaper in the months and years ahead.By the end of this decade most households and schools will be connected to the Net.

Most public schools will have limited funds for staff training in technology, so many students will be ahead of teachers and counselors in their level of knowledge and experience on the Net.

College costs will continue to escalate, making the college-search resources of the Internet more valuable than ever.

You will soon have access to vertical browsers that go out on the Net to find pertinent and specialized college information for you (i.e., the names and Net addresses of the director of admission at X,Y, and Z colleges), which will make your electronic college search a lot less time consuming.

A Special Request

Once you've launched your Web search, using some or all of the techniques suggested in this book, let me know how you're doing. Send me an e-mail message from time to time to let me know about your successes and roadblocks, and any insights that you'd like to pass along, so others can profit from your experience. You can reach me at either of my two e-mail addresses:

inetguide@collegeboard.org
KHart20561@aol.com

Top College Searches on the Web

College Board Online

http://www.collegeboard.org/csearch/html/ch00.html

Connects you to the award-winning ExPAN college search program with a data base of more than 3,000 two-year and four-year colleges. You can choose from among 800 features to create a profile of your ideal college and, in seconds, get a list of the colleges that fit the bill. ExPAN also includes the entire text of the latest edition of *The College Handbook* and lets you complete and submit admission applications online.

CollegeEdge

http://www.collegeedge.com

Search for colleges that match your goals and interests; find useful advice and information on researching, applying, and going to college; have your college application essay reviewed by a former Harvard professor. Chat room and BBS are coming, we're told.

The College Guide

http://www.jayi.com/jayi/ACG/CGTOC.html

This student-oriented site offers electronic links to colleges, admission advice, a searchable data base, and general information about college life. It's part of a larger site targeted at young people's interests.

CollegeNET

http://www.collegenet.com

This is a searchable data base of colleges, scholarship opportunities, and academic resources. It offers a comprehensive college/university index with good graphics and some interesting resources for financial aid and scholarships. The site recently began offering online admission application processing (for featured schools only).

CollegeTown

http://www.ctown.com

A campus quad format lets you visit an admission office, financial aid office, etc. This site provides links to many colleges and offers multimedia portfolios for member institutions. Many of the services promised are still under development.

CollegeView

http://www.collegeview.com

By combining a data base of 3,300 two- and four-year colleges with multimedia tours, CollegeView gives students and parents a general overview of a college, plus a direct e-mail option for requesting additional information.

CollegeXpress

http://www.collegexpress.com

Search colleges by state, major, and a host of other factors. Take a virtual tour of some colleges and ask their experts questions about the college admission process.

FishNet

http://www.jayi.com/ACG/

Get information on colleges via the college search page; create a profile of yourself to send to colleges; ask questions of their admission expert; get information about paying for college; read a collection of articles about college and the admission process.

Internet College Exchange

http://www.usmall.com/college/index.html

With a searchable home page and forums/discussion groups about college life, this site mirrors others on this list. In the future, mailing list, enrollment, and expanded college information will be available. This site has received considerable "hot site" recognition from various Web rating organizations.

Peterson's Education Center

http://www.petersons.com

Peterson's college data base is available on this home page, as is other educational and career information.

The Princeton Review

http://www.review.com

You can search the site by a college's name, region, state, size, and cost. PR also gives you their rating of hundreds of colleges:

http://www.review.com/undergr/best_schools_form.html

Resource Pathways College Information Community

http://www.sourcepath.com

This site offers ranking and "star" evaluations of college admission and financial aid resources, using both paper-based and Internet U.S. News rankings of college admission resources.

Search by Video

http://www.searchbyvideo.com

This company has more than 400 college and boarding school videos available through their Video Library. Each video is $6.

Hispanic Serving Institutions

http://web.fie.com/web/mol

A useful site for identifying colleges that focus on the academic interests and needs of students with Hispanic backgrounds.

Historically Black Colleges and Universities

http://web.fie.com/web/mol

Helps you zero in on institutions with a long tradition of serving the academic needs of African American students.

Ivy League Universities

http://www.artsci.wustl.edu/~jrdorkin/ivy.html

Not much here yet, but it's a shortcut for those interested in the most selective colleges in the country.

Jesuit Colleges and Universities

http://www.ajcunet.edu

AJCUnet helps you search for, link to, and request an application from Jesuit colleges and universities in the United States.

156 National Liberal Arts Colleges

http://www.aavc.vassar.edu/libarts.colleges.html

A list of academic institutions classified by the Carnegie Foundation for the Advancement of Teaching as national liberal arts colleges.

Online Information and Advice About Majors and Careers

Career centers at various universities

http://www.rpi.edu/dept/cdc/carserv

Use this search to locate hundreds of colleges with Web sites that have good career information.

CareerMagazine

http://www.careermag.com

A comprehensive resource, designed to meet the individual needs of networked job seekers.

CareerMosaic

http://www.careermosaic.com

Currently the best single location for information about jobs, internships, and career assessment. Go directly to their College Connection page. Be sure to browse 5-10 college career centers that are hypertext and use their search engines to locate newsgroups.

CareerNet

http://www.careers.org

Links to thousands of career reference sites, organized geographically, alphabetically, and by job family.

Career Planning Process (my personal favorite)

http://www.cba.bgsu.edu/class/webclass/nagye/career/process.html

An online career counselor that encourages users to explore and gather information to enable them to synthesize, gain competencies, make decisions, set goals, and take action. This site is a service of Bowling Green State University.

Career Resource Homepage

http://www.rpi.edu/dept/cdc/homepage.html

Superb link to several commercial data bases. Check out the CyberAlumni option to locate the names and e-mail addresses of professionals in your field of interest.

Career Services

http://www.adm.uwaterloo.ca/infocecs/CRC/manual-home.html

A great online career-interest survey from the University of Waterloo.

Career Talk

http://www.careertalk.com

A weekly syndicated column on the Internet dedicated to advancing your career. E-mail your job search challenges to Career Talk, where you'll also find a great list of other career sites.

CareerWEB

http://www.cweb.com

An easy-to-use, interactive online service that offers employers, franchisers, and career-related companies a chance to reach qualified candidates worldwide and, at the same time, offers qualified candidates the opportunity to browse career opportunities.

Choosing a Major: Factors to Consider

http://www.sas.upenn.edu/college/major/factors_to_consider.html

This site, a service of the University of Pennsylvania, provides a checklist of some key factors to consider when choosing an academic major.

College Board Online

http://www.collegeboard.org

Extensive guidance and information about jobs and careers and how they relate to college majors; part of the comprehensive ExPAN program.

CollegeEdge

http://www.collegeedge.com/CM/CM_HOME.stm

Good information on choosing a major and career, including useful tips and information on college majors, careers, and internships; "day in the life" interviews with people from a wide range of college majors and career areas; and more.

Cornell Career Services

http://www.career.cornell.edu/ccs/Job_Search_Strategies/

Good information on developing career goals and interviewing skills. You'll want to surf this site before your first on-campus interview.

FutureScan Magazine

http://www.futurescan.com

Lets you take a close look at different occupations by reading the profiles of real people in the field and by submitting e-mail questions to working professionals.

JobWeb

http://www.jobweb.org/catapult/career_info.htm

Sponsored by the National Association of Colleges and Employers, this site provides good career planning information—including the Occupational Outlook Handbook, which you can access by clicking on Career Library.

Keirsey Temperament Sorter

http://sunsite.unc.edu/jembin/mb.pl

The Keirsey Temperament Sorter by David Keirsey is a personality test that scores results according to the Meyers-Briggs Inventory system. The actual Meyers-Briggs test is a professional instrument and may be administered only by a licensed practitioner.

The Monster Board Career Center

http://www1.monster.com:80/jobseek/center/ccenter.htm

Online access to over 48,000 jobs, career information, and names/locations of hundreds of employers.

The Online Career Center

http://www.occ.com/occ

One of the first and most comprehensive sites, it includes information about thousands of job and career fairs, advice on resumes, and much more. OCC is unique in that it is sponsored by an association of employers.

Planning a Career

http://www.tgslc.org/adventur/planning.htm

You can get advice on how to choose a career and how to reach your career goal; pick up useful tips on job hunting, resume writing, and job interviewing techniques. This site is a service of Adventures in Education Information Center.

Princeton Review

http://www.review.com/

Search their online data base of career advice for insightful information on hundreds of occupations, internship opportunities, and general advice on interviewing and public speaking.

Scholarly Journals Distributed Via the World-Wide Web

http://info.lib.uh.edu/wj/webjour.html

This directory, accessed through the University of Houston Libraries home page, provides links to established Web-based scholarly journals that offer access to English-language article files without requiring user registration or fees.

Scholarly Societies Project

http://www.lib.uwaterloo.ca/society/webpages.html

Search for and link to the site where professors interact and discuss their disciplines. Look for on-campus e-mail addresses and monitor discussions.

University of Delaware Career Services Center

http://www.udel.edu/CSC/career.html

This office has compiled a "Major Resource Kit" for 49 undergraduate programs. Each "Major Resource Kit" includes information such as entry-level job titles that previous University of Delaware graduates in that program have attained, brief job descriptions, major employers for that field, and listings of professional associations. A great source for networking.

Washington University, St. Louis, Missouri

gopher://gopher.wustl.edu:70/11/WU_Links/Career_Center/majchoose

Includes information on jobs related to a major, help in choosing a job, and access to alumni for career advice. Similar to the University of Delaware site, but not yet as comprehensive.

Finding College Home Pages

Argyle and Navigator Communications

http://www.nav.com/OWR/oneworld.html

Search and link to colleges in more than 40 countries around the world.

Christina DeMello Search

http://www.mit.edu:8001/people/cdemello/univ.html

One of the first and oldest college home page search sites with a data base of more than 3,000 colleges. Has won numerous awards in the past two years.

Colleges and Universities Search

http://www.universities.com

A simple home page search with more than 3,000 colleges in the data base.

Global Computing—American Universities
http://www.globalcomputing.com/universy.html
Direct links to the home pages of more than 700 American universities.

University Pages
http://isl-garnet.uah.edu/Universities_g/
Simple search, by state, sponsored by the University of Alabama at Huntsville.

Yahoo Search (my personal favorite)
http://www.yahoo.com/Regional/Countries/United_States /Education/Colleges_and_Universities
One of the most popular and easiest ways to find and link to a particular college, along with dozens of indexes, including the college's e-mail, departments, and student clubs.

Community and Two-Year Colleges
Take your pick. Here are a few sites where you can search for the home pages of community colleges (and in some cases, four-year colleges) in the United States:
http://www.careermart.com/MMM/communitycolleges.html
http://www.mcli.dist.maricopa.edu/cc/
http://www.utexas.edu/world/comcol.html
http://www.sp.utoledo.edu/twoyrcol.html

Or you can simply conduct a Net search with your browser using the full name of the college or university. In any case, once you've located the college, click on the hypertext name of the institution (typically the color blue) and you're there.

Financial Aid Information

Not-for-Profit Organizations

College Board Online

http://www.collegeboard.org/css/html/save.html

For parents whose children are not yet college age, who are considering adding a savings plan to their current savings and investments, and who want an estimate of how much money they'll have by the time their children enter college, the College Board's College Savings Adviser is the place to go. The analysis is free, instantaneous, and completely secure and confidential.

College Choice Website

http://www.gse.ucla.edu/mm/cc/links/aid.html

Information and links to other financial aid sites, such as ROTC Scholarships, Scholarship Search Services, Index of Minority Scholarships and Fellowships, and Student Loan Information from Banks.

College Funding Company

http://www.collegefundingco.com

Headquartered in Lincoln, Nebraska, the College Funding Company is a coalition of four not-for-profit organizations dedicated to helping families learn about and fund higher education. The site includes general information on financial aid (loans, grants) and a financial aid calculator.

National Association of Student Financial Aid Administrators

http://www.finaid.org

This award-winning site, called FinAid, provides excellent links to Internet sources of information about student financial aid. It is maintained by Mark Kantrowitz, a graduate student at Carnegie-Mellon University. Don't miss this site!

Federal Government

The largest provider of financial aid, the federal government has a great deal of information on student financial aid on its Web site. Here are three good sites to start with:

http://www.ed.gov/offices/OPE/index.html
http://www.ed.gov/prog_info/SFA/StudentGuide
http://easi.ed.gov/index.html

State Governments

More and more state government offices and agencies are coming online. If you're lucky enough to live in the following states, check out their information on financial aid:

California Student Aid Commission: **http://www.csac.ca.gov**

Connecticut Scholarships:
   http://emporium.turnpike.net/R/Rodnet/htfd

Georgia Student Finance Commission: **http://www.gsfc.org**

Maine:
   http://cardinal.umeais.maine.edu/~stuaid/resident.html

New York State: **http://www.hesc.state.ny.us**

Ohio Board of Regents:
   http://www.bor.ohio.gov/progs/obrprog3.html

Vermont Student Assistance Corporation:
   http://www.vsac.org

Commercial Organizations

American Express University

**http://www.americanexpress.com/student/moneypit/
moneypit.html**

American Express's Money Pit has a limited amount of information at this point, but some very practical advice and a helpful calculator.

College Funding Company
http://www.collegefundingco.com
A for-profit company that offers an online questionnaire to counsel families on their Estimated Family Contribution (EFC) and how to reduce it.

Don't Miss Out: The Ambitious Student's Guide to Financial Aid
http://www.signet.com/collegemoney/
An online edition of Robert and Anna Leider's classic book, now in its 20th edition and still one of the better sources of financial aid information available.

Peterson's Education Center
http://www.petersons.com/resources/finance.html
Here you'll find links to organizations (mostly banks) that provide information on how to pay for your education and advice on juggling family finances while any family member is attending college.

Resource Pathways College Information Community
http://www.sourcepath.com
This site's College Financial Aid Resources area attempts to cover all the Web sites on financial aid and link them in a one-stop-shop search.

College Board Online College Money PLANNER

http://www.collegeboard.org/css/html/planform.html

The College Board makes it easy to plan for your financial needs by using the College Money PLANNER Form. The cost for your personalized and comprehensive report is $14.95 and can be completed online and billed directly to your credit card.

DCB&T Financial Planning Calculator

http://www.dcbt.com/FinCalc/College.html

Another calculator for early financial planning, compliments of Douglas County Bank & Trust Co.

Merrill Lynch Personal Finance Center

http://www.merrill-lynch.ml.com/personal/college/ collegecalc.html

Parents, want to know how much it will cost to send your son or daughter to college? Fill out Merrill Lynch's online questionnaire/calculator and wait for your answer.

Wall Street Financial, Inc. College Investment Planner

http://www.wallstreetfinancial.com/college.htm

This site has 1994-95 costs for more than 200 colleges and universities and will provide you with a "realistic view of the costs and benefits" if your fill out their online questionnaire.

Bank Loans

Most commercial banks are coming online and many offer student loan processing. Here are a few:

Citibank: **http://www.citibank.com/student/undergrd.htm**

KeyBank: **http://www.keybank.com/educate.htm**

Nellie Mae Loan Link: **http://www.nelliemae.org**

PNC Bank Corp: **http://www.eduloans.pncbank.com**

Sallie Mae: **http://www.salliemae.com**

Signet Bank: **http://www.signet.com/collegemoney**

Private Scholarships

College Board Online

http://www.collegeboard.org

You can complete a personal profile outlining your background and interests and the FUND FINDER program will quickly—and at no charge—match your qualifications with the requirements for a wide range of scholarships, grants, internships, and loans in the College Board's authoritative, annually updated, online data base. The program gives you a list of funding sources and detailed information about how to apply.

fastWEB

http://www.fastweb.com

A data base of scholarships, grants, fellowships, and loans in private sector funding for college students living in the United States, plus extensive information about federal government financial aid.

Nerd World Media

http://www.nerdworld.com/nw1178.html
An index of sites on the Web that offer financial assistance, grants, loans, and more.

Ethnic and Minority Scholarships

Armenian Students' Association of America

http://www.asainc.org
The Armenian Students' Association, a nonprofit organization, provides scholarships to students.

Hispanic Educational Foundation (HEF)

http://www.nmt.edu/~larranag/hef/hef.html
The HEF offers scholarships at a local level and currently only in the states of Arizona, California, Colorado, Illinois, Kansas, Michigan, Nebraska, New Mexico, Oklahoma, Texas, Utah, Washington, and Washington, DC.

Minority Online Information Service (MOLIS)

http://web.fie.com/web/mol/user.htm
Link to Historically Black Colleges and Universities (HBCUs)and Hispanic-Serving Institutions (HSIs); contact the right people within the minority education community; discover federal minority opportunities; identify scholarships and fellowships.

Commercial Online Services

AOL key word college board>Paying for College
AOL key word real life>Education
AOL key word rsp>Money for Study>Undergraduate
CompuServe: go college>Funding and Finances
CompuServe: go stufob>Browse Libraries>Admissions/Financing

Other Sources

Newspapers and Magazines Online (*Money Magazine, U.S. News, USA Today*). Search the publication's archives using key words (college financial aid, for example) to find articles and columns that offer free advice.

Don't forget to use the SEARCH option on your Web browser. Use key words like: financial aid, college scholar-ships, etc. to find many helpful resources.

Useful Off-Campus Web Sites

American School Counselors Association (ASCA)

http://www.edge.net/asca/

This site provides a listing of high school guidance pages on the Web—each with good information on colleges, careers, and financial aid.

American Society of Association Executives (ASAE)

http://www.asaenet.org

Check out ASAE's rapidly growing "Gateway to Associations," the Internet's largest searchable data base of association Web sites. Locate the association that represents your area of interest, and surf its site for information, e-mail names, and addresses. It's a great location to find a Net pal.

Black Excel

http://www.cnct.com/home/ijblack/BlackExcel.html

A Web site that provides information about predominantly black colleges. Help with college selection, admission, scholarships, and financial aid is available.

The Chronicle of Higher Education

http://www.chronicle.com

This is the major paper for news about higher education issues and concerns. You can search past editions for stories involving a particular college or general topics. Without a valid password (given to paid subscribers only), you're limited in what you can access, but it's still worth surfing for general news on their home page.

College Fair News

http://www.nacac.com/faird&l.html

This is where college admission professionals, including high school college counselors, go to interact with their peers. Dates and locations of the NACAC National College Fairs can be found at this site. Apart from that information, this site focuses exclusively on the interests and needs of college admission professionals.

College Newspapers

http://www.linkmag.com/news/CNEWS.html

This site contains a listing and link to online college newspapers in America. Read each paper of interest—some let you search past editions by subject (e.g., crime on campus).

Greek Pages

http://www.greekpages.com

A listing of national and local chapters of fraternities and sororities sorted by college and by organization. A good source for e-mail. Once you have one name and address you can ask that your e-mail be forwarded to other members of the organization—including students in your intended major.

Hillel

http://www.hillel.org

Jewish students can find information about colleges with Hillel chapters. Use the directory to e-mail the campus director at each college you're interested in, requesting the e-mail address of other Jewish students on campus.

University Links

http://www-net.com/univ

A resource for college-bound students, teachers, parents, and counselors.

USNews Online—School Rankings

http://www.USNEWS.com/usnews/fair/natuniv.htm

In looking at how USNEWS ranks colleges, keep in mind that "best" for one student may not be for another, so the information you glean here should be only one of the many factors that play a role in deciding where to apply.

World Alumni Net

http://www.infophil.com/World/Alumni

Here's one location where you can find the names of alumni and alumni organizations all over the world. Find the colleges that interest you and surf for e-mail addresses.

World Lecture Hall (WLH)

http://www.utexas.edu/world/lecture

WLH contains links to pages created by faculty worldwide who are using the Web to deliver class materials. For example, you will find course syllabi, assignments, lecture notes, exams, class calendars, multimedia textbooks, etc. Use this site to network with faculty.

World News Index

http://www.stack.urc.tue.nl/~haroldkl/index.html

This is an index of national and local newspapers. It contains links to almost all the daily news providers on the World Wide Web. Go to the newspaper in the city or town where a college that interests you is located to read about current and past events off campus.

Glossary

Address: On the Internet, your address is made up of two main sections identifying who you are and where you are located. The common format is who@where.type of domain (see domain). For example, the address khartman@collegeboard.org means: Ken Hartman at the College Board, which, as a nonprofit organization, is identified as org.

Bits Per Second: Unit of measure that refers to the speed at which data can be transmitted.

Bookmarks (see Hotlist)

Browser: Refers to a mechanism that enables users to search for and explore Web sites on the Internet. Netscape is an example of a browser.

Bulletin Board Service (BBS): An electronic forum on the Internet or on a commercial online service for users to browse and exchange information by posting messages and responding to other people's messages. Bulletin boards, also called message boards, are often organized by topic in electronic folders.

Chat Room: Chat rooms offer real-time conferencing among subscribers to an online service. Two or more people in a chat room area at the same time "talk" to each other by typing their comments and ideas back and forth as they would do in conversation. A chat room differs from a BBS, which doesn't provide for immediate, interactive exchanges among a group of people.

Commercial Online Service: A company that, for a fee, provides computer users with electronic access to information and services via a modem and phone line. Examples are America Online, Microsoft Network, CompuServe, and Prodigy.

Cyberspace: A word coined to describe the networks of computers that enable people to communicate with others throughout the world simultaneously and almost instantaneously.

Data Base: A storehouse of information on a given subject—undergraduate colleges, for example, or nationwide airline schedules, or careers—that is stored electronically and can be searched via a computer.

Dedicated Line: A telephone or cable line that is connected directly to the Internet for the fastest access to content on the Net.

Dial-Up Internet Connection: Lets a user dial into an Internet service provider using a modem and telephone line to access the Internet. The user is presented with a text-based set of menus to use in navigating among sites on the Internet (see SLIP or PPP).

Directory: A list of files (names of people, products, data bases, etc.) that can be accessed at an Internet site.

Domain: This is the part of an Internet address that identifies the type of organization. All Internet addresses include one of six domains:

.com   commercial organization
.net   networks
.org   nonprofit/not-for-profit organization
.gov   federal government
.edu   educational institution
.mil   unclassified military network

Download/Upload: Download is to transfer a file from another computer to the user's computer. Upload is to input a file so that it can be accessed by the user or others.

E-Mail: A system that enables computer users to send messages to other users via an electronic network.

File Transfer Protocol (FTP): Allows files to be transferred between Internet-connected computers.

Flaming: Sending an angry or nasty message to another person in a newsgroup or bulletin board on the Internet.

Frequently Asked Questions (FAQ): A file of answers to questions frequently asked about a wide range of Internet and Web-related topics. FAQ files are available at many locations on the Net and save you the time you'd spend posting a question and waiting for a response.

Gopher: A menu-based information-retrieval tool for accessing data bases, text files, and other resources on the Internet.

Graphical User Interface (GUI): Software that lets Internet users execute commands by pointing and clicking on words or phrases with a mouse.

Home Page: The first page of a Web site, which acts as a table of contents to that site and provides an overview of what the site has to offer.

Hotlist (also known as Bookmarks): A personal list of favorite and frequently used Web addresses. All Web browsers have a function that lets users create hotlists/bookmarks so they can return easily and quickly to their favorite Web sites.

HTML (Hypertext Markup Language): Programming language used to develop and display information on the Web.

HTTP (Hypertext Transport Protocol): The computer language that enables browser software and Web sites to transmit information back and forth.

Hyperlink/Hypertext: An underlined word, phrase, or graphic on a Web page that you can click on with a mouse to go immediately to a related piece of information elsewhere on the Internet.

Internaut: Anyone who uses the Internet.

Internet: The global "network of networks" that connects millions of computers and enables users to communicate in a growing variety of ways.

Internet Account: An Internet account, obtained through an Internet provider, gives you a password and e-mail address to use on the Internet.

Internet Relay Chat (IRC): Interactive, real-time discussions in the form of text messages between Internet users.

Internet Server: A computer that stores data that can be accessed via the Internet.

Internet Service Provider (ISP): Any organization that provides access to the Internet. Many ISPs also offer technical help to subscribers, and several of them offer a wide range of the sort of information and entertainment features you find on the Web.

Internet Site: Any computer connected to the Internet that

provides information that can be accessed using an Internet navigation tool.

IP (Internet Protocol) Address: The unique number assigned to each computer on the Internet.

ISDN (Integrated Services Digital Network): A fast Internet connection available through local cable and telephone companies.

Java: A programming language that enables Web sites to present animation and other special effects.

Key Word: A word or words used by a search engine to locate documents or menus.

Listserv (Mailing List): A form of one-to-many communication using e-mail. Being part of a listserv is something like subscribing to a magazine, except that it's free and the "articles" are the messages exchanged by the subscribers. Subscribers discuss issues in their field, solicit advice, coordinate action, and share information. There are currently more than 4,000 listservs that can be read and posted to.

Log On: To sign on to a computer system.

Menu: A list of subjects that leads you to documents or other menus.

Message Board (see Bulletin Board Service)

Modem: An electronic device that links a computer to the online world via a phone line. Modems are available for any computer, can be internal or external, and come in several speeds, known as baud rates.

Netscape: A popular, easy-to-use Web browser, available for both Mac and Windows.

Net Surfer: Someone who browses the Internet with no definite destination.

Network: Two or more computers connected electronically so that people using them can share files and exchange e-mail. Special types of networks include local area networks (LANs) and wide area networks (WANs).

Newbie: A newcomer to the Internet.

Newsgroups: Usenet message areas, organized by topic, where users can read and respond to messages from other members in that group. Newsgroups are similar to discussion groups on a BBS.

Online/Offline: You are online when your computer is connected by modem to the Internet. You're offline when your computer isn't connected to a network by modem.

Post: Send e-mail messages to a listserv, BBS, or Usenet newsgroup to be read by subscribers or others on the Internet.

Secure Socket Layer: A new device developed by credit card companies to ensure secure exchange of information, such as credit card numbers, on the Internet.

SLIP (Serial Line Internet Protocol) or PPP (Point to Point Protocol): Internet connections that let you navigate the Web using a graphical browser, such as Mosaic, in contrast to a dial-up connection, which limits you to a text-based browser.

Smiley: Type elements used to indicate a particular emotion. The two most commonly used are :) to indicate happy and :(to indicate sad.

TCP/IP (Transmission Control Protocol/Internet Protocol): The programs that govern communications among computers on the Internet.

Telnet: An Internet program that lets you connect with other Internet computers and access their data.

URL (Universal Resource Locator): The address and method used to locate a specific resource on the Internet. A URL beginning with http:// indicates that a site is a Web resource and that a Web browser must be used to access it.

Usenet Newsgroups: More than 20,000 topic-oriented message bases that can be read and posted to.

Virtual: A computer-generated environment.

WWW: Abbreviation for the World Wide Web.

WAIS (**Wide Area Information Servers**): These servers enable users to conduct full-text key word searches in documents, data bases, and libraries connected to the Internet.

Web: Short for World Wide Web.

Web Browser: Software that lets Internet users access and navigate the World Wide Web.

Web Page: An online hypertext document containing information that can be accessed over the World Wide Web.

World Wide Web (WWW or Web): An Internet browsing system that allows for point-and-click navigation of the Internet. The WWW is an interconnection of millions of pieces of information in text and multimedia form located on computers around the world.

Yahoo: A popular search engine that combines a subject index listing and a Web searching program. You can access Yahoo on the Internet at http://www.yahoo.com.

Index